Coyote Kills John Wayne

Reencounters with Colonialism:
New Perspectives on the Americas

Mary C. Kelley, AMERICAN HISTORY, DARTMOUTH COLLEGE

Agnes Lugo-Ortiz, LATIN AMERICAN STUDIES, DARTMOUTH COLLEGE

Donald Pease, AMERICAN LITERATURE, DARTMOUTH COLLEGE

Ivy Schweitzer, AMERICAN LITERATURE, DARTMOUTH COLLEGE

Diana Taylor, LATIN AMERICAN AND LATINO STUDIES, NEW YORK UNIVERSITY

Frances R. Aparicio and Susana Chávez-Silverman, eds., *Tropicalizations: Transcultural Representations of Latinidad*

Michelle Burnham, *Captivity and Sentiment: Cultural Exchange in American Literature, 1682–1861*

Colin G. Calloway, ed., *After King Philip's War: Presence and Persistence in Indian New England*

Carla Gardina Pestana and Sharon V. Salinger, *Inequality in Early America*

Renée L. Bergland, *The National Uncanny: Indian Ghosts and American Subjects*

Susana Rotker, *The American Chronicles of José Martí Journalism and Modernity in Spanish America*

Carlton Smith, *Coyote Kills John Wayne: Postmodernism and Contemporary Fictions of the Transcultural Frontier*

COYOTE KILLS JOHN WAYNE

POSTMODERNISM AND CONTEMPORARY FICTIONS OF THE TRANSCULTURAL FRONTIER

Carlton Smith

DARTMOUTH COLLEGE

Published by University Press of New England / Hanover and London

Dartmouth College

Published by University Press of New England, Hanover, NH 03755

© 2000 by Carlton Smith

Printed in the United States of America   5   4   3   2   1

Portions of this manuscript previously appeared in earlier essays by Carlton Smith, notably in "Arctic Revelations: Vollmann's Rifles and the Frozen Landscape of the Self." *The Review of Contemporary Fiction*, summer 1993, Volume 13, No. 2, and in "Coyote, Contingency and Community: Thomas King's *Green Grass, Running Water* and Postmodern Trickster." *American Indian Quarterly*, summer 1997, Volume 21, No. 3.

Library of Congress Cataloging-in-Publication Data
Smith, Carlton, 1956–
    Coyote kills John Wayne: postmodernism and contemporary fictions of the trans-cultural frontier / Carlton Smith.
        p.   cm.   (Reencounters with colonialism—new perspectives on the Americas)
    Includes index.
        ISBN 1–58465–019–2 (alk. paper)—ISBN 1–58465–020–6 (pbk. : alk. paper)
        1. American fiction—20th century—History and criticism.   2. Frontier and pioneer life in literature.   3. American fiction—West (U.S.)—History and criticism.   4. Pluralism (Social sciences) in literature.   5. Postmodernism (Literature)—West (U.S.).   6. Western stories—History and criticism.   7. Culture conflict in literature.   8. West (U.S.)—In litera-ture.   9. Ethnic groups in literature.   10. Minorities in literature.   I. Title.   II. Series.
PS374.F73 S65   2000
813'.54093278—dc21   99–49692

For Deborah,

without whom there would be no book, no moon, no heaven . . .

Contents

Acknowledgments

In writing *Coyote Kills John Wayne*, I have benefited immeasurably from various forms of institutional support, as well as from the innumerable and invaluable conversations with colleagues, friends, and family members. Generous support from the University of California's president's postdoctoral fellowship afforded me time to writet and also allowed me to spend two important years at the University of California at Irvine's Humanities Research Institute. I need to thank, as well, the Center for Ideas and Society, located at the University of California's Riverside campus, for their fellowship and support. This grant enabled me to spend three interesting months with Gayatri Chakavorty Spivac as she reminded us all how important it is "to pay our dues" by combining serious inquiry with a commitment to praxis.

I remember with gratitude and regret my former teacher, the late Brian Moore.

As a graduate student at the University of California, Riverside, I had many stimulating discussions regarding aspects of the ideas explored in this book. Special thanks to Katherine Kinney and Geoff Cohen, whose continuing emotional and intellectual support means more than I can ever say. Thanks too to Richard Boyd who made numerous helpful suggestions along the way, not the least of which was to quit playing so much golf. George Haggerty, Joseph Childers, Carole-Anne Tyler, Susan Foster, Mike Krekorian, Milton Miller, John Ganim, Parama Roy, Marguerite Waller, Steven Axelrod, and Georgia Elliott all provided timely suggestions and created a resonant, creative, intellectual climate. I am also appreciative of the fellowships and assistantships provided by the university.

I thank persistently and inadequately Emory Elliott, who represents the best in our profession. His dedication to making the field more representative of cultural and intellectual diversity has done more for the right cause than most of us will ever be able to contemplate. My thanks, Emory, for your commitment to difference and multivalent voices.

A number of critical perspectives influenced some of the ideas explored in *Coyote Kills John Wayne*, not the least of which are those of John Carlos Rowe, Gerald Vizenor, Louis Owens, and Larry McCaffery. Thanks to these scholars for the important and invaluable critical perspectives their work has provided.

I've also benefited from the discourse of my colleagues at Palomar College and been inspired by their mutual devotion to teaching and scholarship. In particular I thank Barbara Neult Kelber, Anne Holman, Brent Gowen, Ann Maioroff, Pam McDonough, Fergal O'Doherty, Charles Ingham, and Dan Finkenthal as well as the college for its institutional support.

I'd like to acknowledge the work and vision of Naida Garcia, who struggles against a range of forces to keep classes and hope alive at Palomar College's Pauma Valley Reservation Educational Center. She has steadily assisted me in my work at the center.

I express my deep gratitude to Cindi Spencer and John Goldsworthy, who kindly overlooked my profound lack of computer skills and have patiently assisted me in the preparation of this manuscript.

I have also been fortunate to have friends and family who sustained me in the years that I worked on this book, people who listened to my ranting and often provided salutary suggestions and editorial assistance. Wayne and Gloria Smith, Marion Smith, Dianna and Spencer Woodbury, Tim and Serena Powers, Bob Driscoll, Paul and Robert and Maria Rohrer, and, of course, Samantha and Benjamin Hatheway all contributed greatly to this effort.

April Ossmann, at the University of New England Press, has not only provided expert editorial guidance but has been unfailingly thoughtful in her help and responses. I benefited too from the insights provided by all those who reviewed and commented upon the manuscript.

Finally, I want to thank my colleague and partner, Deborah Paes de Barros, whose profound contributions to this project simply go beyond words.

June 1999   C.S.

Coyote Kills John Wayne

CHAPTER ONE

Postmodern Frontiers: Tales from a Ghost Town

The coarseness and strength combined with acuteness and inquisitiveness; that practical, inventive turn of mind, quick to find expedients; that masterful grasp of material things, in the artistic but powerful to effect great ends; that restless, nervous energy; that dominant individualism, working for good and for evil, and withal that buoyancy and exuberance which comes with freedom—these are the traits of the frontier, or traits called out elsewhere because of the frontier.

—Frederick Jackson Turner,
The Significance of the Frontier in American History

"It's still weird though," said Minnie. "Who would want to kill John Wayne?"   —Thomas King, *Green Grass, Running Water*

Absent Voices

OVER A HUNDRED years ago, Frederick Jackson Turner stood among fellow historians in Chicago at the World's Columbian Exposition of 1893 and delivered his now famous lecture, "The Significance of the Frontier in American History." Outside the elegant conference rooms, away from the bright technological marvels meant to signal the dawning of a new techno-industrial age, Buffalo Bill Cody staged his immensely popular Wild West Show, a spectacle purporting to dramatize the progression of American history and the civilizing of the frontier. Featuring various historical "reen-actments," Cody's show presented a succession of "epochs." Scenes progressed from "woodland dancers," to John Smith and Pocahantas, to "western" settlements, and eventually culminated with Annie Oakley's gun-play and various other acts of "cowboy fun" (Slotkin 63–67).[1] Included among the Indians who participated in this unofficial sideshow on the Chicago Midway were numerous veterans of Wounded Knee, the final battle of the Indian wars.[2]

Inside the exposition itself, however, where Turner would deliver his speech, Indians clearly had little place within the utopian fantasies of a beckoning modernism. Indeed, Turner's speech, like the exposition itself, was remarkable both for what it asserted and what was conspicuously absent. For the gloomy Turner, the American frontier had served as a "safety valve" that not only had allowed for a distinctive American character but also had provided a "hostile" and remote terrain in which American exceptionalism could flourish. Like the railway lines that had scored the landscape, the homesteads, and emergent urban centers such as the metropolis of Chicago, the frontier space had become the repository of an imagined American spirit.[3] For Turner, this exceptionalism was now threatened by the "closing of the American frontier," a condition confirmed by the census of 1890 in which America was deemed completely inhabited. Turner's narrative was both elegiac and cautionary; without the frontier, American individualism might be threatened. It is telling that Turner barely mentioned the Indians of the frontier. For him, they remained invisible, implicitly and ineluctably consumed by the forward progress of America and nation-building.

The virtual nonappearance of Native Americans in Turner's narrative indicates the extent to which Turner's individualism, and with it his conceptions of a singular American "national character," were predicated on an absence. This absence was that of the largely unrepresented Other against which such constructs could be maintained. In this sense, Turner's speech had proven cautionary in an unintended way. Cultural exceptionalism and dominance could only be asserted and defined against the liminal, the historically silenced. Turner's narrative thus reinscribed a familiar set of relations that both preceded and followed it. Like the Columbian Exposition, Turner's narrative offered a vision of America where Others remained outside official representations of what was most American, perhaps spectacular or exotic, but seemingly irrelevant and doomed to disappearance. For generations, Indian stories—along with those of African Americans, women, Chinese, and Mexicans—correspondingly found little voice in mainstream discussions and representations of the American frontier. Rather, representatives of these groups figured in white stories as Others against which notions of "Nation" and "American" could be constructed. Historically, the genealogy of such representations moves from the discovery narratives of DeBaca and Columbus through James Fennimore Cooper's frontier romances and the ensuing dime novels. It can be traced to the eventual explosion of filmic images that pitted "true" Americans against a range of "dark" savages. Turner's speech thus inaugurated a kind of cultural monologue, a long history in which pop culture became the refractory point for oppressive colonialist allegories.[4]

Presently, viewed from within the interpretive frame of postmodernism, our awareness of the world as ever-constructed has shed new light on such categories as "the frontier" and "civilization." The very idea of a West presupposes a set of relations. So, too, the notion of the West posits the very idea of a frontier and borders. That these borders are but arbitrary constructions makes them no less important to examinations of the West and frontier literature. Slippery, problematic, and mobile, borders remain as ethnic, personal, and nationalized spaces, which require negotiation.

Leslie Silko's work has been marked by her attention to the cultural significance of borders, and the texts and voices that speak at its margins. Silko's "Private Property" probes the nature of borders and barriers, and the concept of ownership, which must inevitably result. In the story, told by an orphaned-child narrator who can only imperfectly negotiate the space of the other villagers' campfires, a group of wild and beautiful horses constantly stampede and tear down the neighbors' fences. It is impossible to contain the horses because although they "belong" to the character Cheromiah, "the horses don't know [or recognize] that."

Similarly, the fences that Etta insists on building are metaphorically violated by the other characters. Too many years of living with "white people" in Winslow have made Etta forget that "we only make use of these things. We don't own them. Nobody owns anything." The conclusion of the story forces both Etta and the reader to confront the meaningless of borders, as well as the fact that they will be consistently constructed and eradicated, leaving "rusty wire and fence posts trailing behind like a broken necklace" ("Private Property," 371). Similarly, Silko's *Almanac of the Dead* (which will be dealt with at much greater length later in this text) maintains that there are no real borders save those of sensibility. For Silko, borders are European and corrosive constructions whose shifting parameters the marginalized inhabitants and the "mixed breeds" must comprehend and subvert.

In his powerful study of the appropriation and poisoning of Native American lands, *If You Poison Us: Uranium and Native Americans*, author Peter Eichstaedt investigates the ways in which Indian land in the Southwest has been historically exploited. Argues Eichstaedt, "the land, the Indians believed, belonged to no one. Man was simply one of its temporary occupants. The concept of a single person 'owning' or buying a piece of land was not only alien and bizarre to the Indians, it was laughable" (Eichstaedt 14). Without the concept of ownership, borders did not apply. But the Anglo-European belief in the existence of borders (coupled with a belief in the implicit right to violate these same borders) has largely defined the history of the frontier. If, as Turner had noted with alarm, the borders defining the frontier as "us" and "them" have disappeared, they have also been internalized and thus become part of the deep structure of our symbolic and discursive landscape.

The frontier is the space from within which the very concept of borders and their corresponding margins have been traditionally disputed and simultaneously explored. Historically, a great deal of literature has attested to this point; the corridas of the Southwest, the worksongs of the Chinese laborers engaged in building the transcontinental railroads, and the private diaries of pioneer women all describe the not mutually exclusive desire to both describe and violate the parameters of frontier life. Perhaps the most notable example of this process is found in the work of Mourning Dove, whose novel, *Cogewa, the Half Blood* (1927), records the perpetual negotiation performed by the "go-between people" as they explore the borderlands. The first novel to be written and published by an Indian woman, *Cogewa* tells the story of a "mixed-blood" Okanogan, orphan girl, whose Anglo father has deserted the family to search for gold in the frozen Northwest. Cogewa inhabits a ranch wherein the cinema-style cowboys are really Indians. Born during the last years of the Indian wars, educated at a mission school and later at a secretarial program in Calgary, and ultimately reconnected with tribal life because of her intense interest in protecting Native American oral tradition, Mourning Dove's life corresponds to her fictive Cogewa's effort to understand the dialogic identity that belongs to the American Indian.

A story steeped in the tropes of nineteenth-century romantic fiction, *Cogewa* has enjoyed a mixed reception. Few copies sold at the time of its initial publication, and even today the heavily edited and Anglicized text is regarded as a suspect literary hybrid. Nonetheless, as Louis Owens notes in his *Other Destinies: Understanding the American Indian Novel* (1992):

Mourning Dove accomplishes a great deal in this novel, not the least of which are the creation of an independent, forceful, mixed-blood woman and the illumination of the teasing humor that permeates American Indian communities and is universally ignored in writing about Indians. Together with her complex treatment of identity within this "cowboys and Indians" world, these accomplishments underscore Mourning Dove's refusal to succumb to the stereotypes that have informed most writing about American Indians. . . . The conclusion, the dilemma of the mixedblood poised between red and white worlds remains unresolved. . . . The novel ends on a note of stasis, with nothing resolved, none of the many questions answered. (Owens 48)

Mourning Dove's work is significant in that it overtly and covertly addresses that transitional space with which Indian questions of identity are concerned. The novel is necessarily a "hybrid" because it examines the concept of hybrid identity.

In a sense, then, Mourning Dove's work provides a fable for students of the frontier. In Cogewa's world the ranch is owned by a white man, the Anglo-inspired cowboys are "breeds" (given names, for example, like "Celluloid Bill"), Cogewa's suitor (who is also the novel's villain) is white and the novel's hero is the mixed breed, LaGrinder. Moving between worlds, Cogewa exclaims, "I am only a breed." Cogewa's ranch is analogous to the territory of postmodernism; it is the space of hybridity and transitional identities.

So, in light of the shared concerns and vocabulary of frontier and postmodern discourse, it is perhaps not mere coincidence that, today, as we spin what cultural critic Manfredo Tafuri has called "the fable of postmodernism," the American fables of the frontier have enjoyed a renewed popularity. Indeed, since 1970, American popular culture has produced a vast array of western museums, wild-west theme restaurants, and frontier fashion (à la Ralph Lauren), while the 1980s and early 90s were marked by the proliferation of television and cinematic westerns as well as the widespread urban acceptance of country western music.[5] And this newly "discovered," newly merchandized frontier was not lauded only in the United States; in Italy the spaghetti western has flourished since the 1960s, while in Japan western music has become a mainstay of nightclubs and bars. No longer the sole province of John Wayne, the western and frontier landscape is explored in new and frequently parodic and ironic ways.[6] All of this cultural production suggests a revived interest in a frontier past, and perhaps more significantly a renewed anxiety about notions of "discovery," colonization, and borders. But this cultural work also alludes to, however unconsciously, the diologic conversation that links this nearly millennial moment with the final days of the frontier.

Just as the cartographers of the "old" west sought to map out and explain the shifting territory of the frontier, postmodern theorists seek to define the shifting epistemological terrain that comprises the contemporary world. But while traditional discovery narratives attempted to justify as well as reveal, much of postmodern criticism struggles to reconstitute an alternative historic memory. For each group the task proves problematic.

Curiously, in spite of the monolithic projections of the frontier by men such as Turner, ultimately the West was defined by its lack of discernible borders, by the inadequacy of signs, by the blurred and ill-defined nature of its dusty trails, and by a vast and echoing absence. Similarly, in both its popular and its arcane and linguistic forms, postmodernism must address finally what cannot be represented. The traditional western attempted to find self-definition by reflecting its concerns off of the refractory image of the Other. But, because this Other was always ultimately a mirror—a projected fantasy about the self—these attempts were largely unsatisfactory. This same projection frequently can be discerned in popular culture.

The fear of the "savage" Other—immigrants, global terrorists, disenfranchised Russians, and of course extraterrestrials—occupies a primary position within contemporary film, television, novels, and even talk radio. In this sense, it is not surprising that so much of postmodern literature takes place in the cyber realm of science fiction and is concerned with the humanoid, the cloned, and the extraterrestrial, as all of these constructions provide metaphors for the Other. What we watch is an interrogation of borders and self. But there are other intersections between the older "discovery" narratives and postmodernism.

Why this insistent pairing of postmodern criticism with marginalized texts? Is not this theoretical insistence yet another heavy-handed appropriation of the Other by the European? While this criticism must be addressed—even acknowledged—I maintain that these two discourses speak to one another. While postmodern theory may provide a critical vocabulary with which to interrogate certain marginalized texts, much more significantly, these same marginalized texts provide example and vitality for what some might regard as the overly cerebral, tiredly European errand of postmodernity. But postmodernism merely explicates what the Other has actually demonstrated. Thus, Derrida explains the arcane mysteries of absence, trace, and the slippery possibilities of presence. But the trickster—favored trope of Native American literature—actually performs these sleight of hands. The texts speak—perform—the same lexicon.

History, remarks Tafuri, is a production of the Lacanian imaginary. The work of this imaginary is important when considering the very notion of the frontier. The dialogic interrogation of this idea probes the process of how the imaginary constructs history and how this mythic history comes to construct the possibility of American identity.

Regarded by Europeans as mongrels and largely ahistorical, the inhabitants of the frontier space possessed an anxious imaginary, restlessly seeking some identity.[7] Frontier fables provided this identity through the production of a homogeneous, "westering" American who was defined by his ability to silence the frightening persona of the Other. In this way, erasing as it did everyone except his white male subject, Turner's credo of the frontier made the western border space emblematic of the "American character." Turner thus interred the colonized Other as a kind of historic backdrop and bit of visual scenery for the central drama he would inscribe.

The creation of a historic, national identity demanded the creation of a kind of semiotic code. From coonskin hats, to log cabins, to guns, this newly forged identity used a specific vocabulary. Interwoven with the American mythos was the vocabulary and sign system equated with the Other—dark skin, feathers, tomahawks, and an incomprehensible language. Similarly, as Linda Hutcheon argues in *Textual Practice* (19), confronted as it is with the constructed nature of history, postmodernism is forced to "rethink" or re-remember history, borrowing the semiotic systems of the past but arranging them in alternative patterns. The mapping of history is revealed as both arbitrary and illusory.

In the process of this remapping, the trope of the frontier has come into stark relief within the context of postmodernism. Marked as it is by epistemological and ontological uncertainty, an incredulity toward metanarrative and an unyielding inquiry into the relationships between power and representation, postmodernism shares with frontier texts a concern with what Hutcheon terms the "inescapably political" and the "resolutely historical."

Because of its highly visible and concrete nature, contemporary architecture provides a cogent allegory for the postmodern comprehension of historic memory. What Jameson refers to as "alternative cognitive mapping" can be clearly viewed in the deconstructive/postmodern design of the late 1970s and 80s.[8] Meditating on the semiotic play of contemporary architecture McHale notes that "no fully satisfactory cognitive mapping of the late-capitalist world-system, it would appear, has yet been achieved . . . [but] to date, the most successful attempts have been in architecture" (McHale 177). The tropes of this attempted mapping are clear; broken, de-centered lines contextualize historic referents. The buildings are filled with classical columns, Roman arches, the barbed wire webs of the southwestern border, the technological bricolage of the postindustrial apocalypse, and, strangely, the false fronts and exaggerated facades frequently associated with "the Old West." It may be that this fascination is logical.

Bodi, Lodi, Rhyolite and Calico, and a thousand other ghost towns mark the west. As our predilection for nostalgia grows, these deserted towns are photographed and visited with an increasing frequency. They appear oddly familiar. The free-standing walls made from concrete and mud, and dotted with sun-stained purple glass, the bolts of rusted barbed wire, the false fronts reminiscent of a Hollywood sound stage, and the small, often crooked windows are referenced by contemporary design. They also simultaneously expose our own mythic and unconscious recollection of what we have privileged as traces of the elusive past. In the ghost town, small signs draw attention to the spaces inhabited by the Other. The "Chinese Camp" and even sometimes a small house of prostitution located some distance away from the other buildings are marked. "Boot Hill," the dilapidated graveyard and site of the sleeping ghosts, are duly noted. Some of the shacks are still filled with decaying bedrolls and kitchen accoutrements. On the ground are discarded items, bottles, animal traps, and mining equipment. Something has happened here, the site seems to say, while the guidebook spins a narrative about depleted mines and falling silver prices. These spaces are familiar because postmodern architects have borrowed from and reproduced them.

But most significantly, the floating historic flotsam can be read as the world after the apocalypse—ill-defined, filled with articles that have lost their narrative anchor, semiotic signs without a correlative. The postapocalyptic quality is integral to what it means to be a ghost town. The ghost town becomes the signifier that marks the place of the irrecoverable and perhaps even nonexistent past. Like the discursive terrain of postmodernism, and like the dilapidated miner's cabin in Bodi, the frontier marks the space of this temporal fracture. It is the space of continuously reforged and renegotiated identity.

Students of either the frontier's texts and border and "discovery" stories, or explorers of the postmodern are left then with what might be viewed as an abandoned and even fantastic hacienda—simulacra which have displaced any "real" history. From within this dilapidated hacienda—a *rancho*, if you will, that is not so different from the ranch inhabited by Mourning Dove's Cogewa—narratives, fictions, and historic explanations evolve. The ruptures elude understanding and collapse into still further projections and simulacra. Like the designer using the mise-en-abîme—the mirror or mural that only reflects the fantastic invention of the interior space and the imaginary—our own narratives are caught within the distorted vocabulary of earlier fables. There is no way out of this historic space. Turner's mythic history as well as Mourning Dove's story shape our vocabulary.

Like Mourning Dove's Cogewa, we are imprisoned within the fictive *rancho* of temporal, racial, and spacial hybridity. Like Mourning Dove, we must read what is hidden within the texts of the frontier and the border, and understand that they are necessarily polyvocal. The postmodernist is self-conscious, and so, like Cogewa, we acknowledge the structures and discourses of power and try to recall the repressed memories and histories of the Other. But we are only marginally successful, because even these alternative histories are in some way structured by the language of the past. The result is an intersection of fables, fables that seek to erase one another and are finally interdependent and must share the same lexicon. Like Mourning Dove, we are left with semiotic play, left with the self-conscious celluloid *rancho*. Like Cogewa, we too are hybrids.

The texts explored in this book can be conceived of as tales from the deserted *rancho*. They are rooted in the vocabulary and images of discovery and frontier literature. But they are by no means "discovery" narratives or westerns in the traditional sense. Rather, they represent attempts to understand the world—to understand how it has traditionally been constructed and to offer an alternate memory to the problematic history of the Americas. These texts resist Turner's monochromatic thesis, yet, like postmodern architecture, they replicate the tropes of frontier discourse. They present for the reader, finally, an alternate space of borders and "discovery," and as readers reflect backwards, they inevitably stumble upon the distorted images and fantasies of "history" and fable.

Situated in this way, as imaged in the texts in *Coyote Kills John Wayne*, the frontier provides not so much a stable place but, rather, a mutable terrain that engenders a variety of postmodern critiques. In this regard, the texts assembled here suggest an underlying argument implicit in *Coyote Kills John Wayne*. Postmodernism here emerges not so much as a historical epoch, or a style of presentation, in the sense that Fredric Jameson asserts in *The Political Unconscious*, but rather as what I would argue is a strategy of representation that foregrounds representational systems and their ability to make epistemological and ontological claims. In this regard they implicitly engage in what many have called the "rhetoric of rupture," a rhetoric whose tropes often include the familiar marks of the postmodern: the absence of center, free play, *jouissance*, and always an ironic distance.

But beyond, these ruptured tropes allude to the important way in which the decay of master narratives implicit in Turner's definition of America has eroded within the shadows of poststructuralist interventions. Taken from this perspective, the texts in this volume often exhibit versions of postmodernisms closer to that of François Lyotard in *Just Gaming*. As Lyotard writes:

[I]t is because one "hams" it up, because one invents, because one inserts novel episodes that stand out as motifs against the narrative plot line . . . that [narrative/storytelling] is successful. When we say tradition, we think identity without difference, whereas there actually is very much difference: the narratives get repeated but are never identical . . . narratives must be repeated all the time because they are forgotten all the time. But what does not get forgotten is the temporal beat. . . . Tradition needs to be rethought. (33–34)

For Lyotard, the "pagan" and the postmodern sensibility are defined by their refusal to accept a centralized narrative order, and by the sense that story and narrative—even story and narrative that seem somehow situated within a larger "tradition"—are about the continual, dynamic reconstitution of narrative rather than its accurate repetition.

Of course, at this particular historic moment, we are engaged in what the political right has chosen to call "the culture wars." The resulting debate and backlash resonate with Turner's thesis and his argument that national identity has much to do with borders. Many individuals have suggested that the desire to define American character as a chronic resistance to the border-occupying Other is both a transhistorical trope and a bitter condition of American cultural life. But the postmodern moment seems preoccupied with the ideas of identity and border. This preoccupation suggests that frontier history and postmodernism share some mutual concerns.

In her essay "Histories, Empires and the Post-Colonial Moment," critic Catherine Hall contends that the "postmodern moment" is shaped by these continuing and pervasive questions regarding identity and borders. The seeming contradiction, presented by the agenda of the new globalism and increased demands of regionalism and localism, frames our contemporary discourse in a manner that is not so different from the ways in which the vying territories of the frontier struggled within the confinement of a larger national narrative. Ponders Hall:

In the late twentieth century, questions about cultural identity seem to have become critical everywhere. "Who are we?" "Where do we come from?" "Which 'we' are we talking about when we talk about 'we'?" Such questions are always there, intimately connected to but distinct from the insistent questions of origins that engage every child, but they have new salience in the contemporary moment. (Chambers/Curti 65)

Living among the wreckage and traces of imperial history and grand narrative, the postcolonial subject must rethink and re-remember history, forging new identities and new definitions of cultural identity. This task must occupy both the colonized and the colonizer; both are "linked through their histories, histories which are forgotten in the desire to throw off the embarrassing reminders" (Hall 66). From the diaspora of history, new myths and fictions are inscribed. This task is defined within the fiction of those writing from the margins of the frontier and within the discourse of postmodernism.

As postmodern authors have mined the territory of "discovery" literature and frontier narrative, they have sought not merely to reinscribe and recodify traditional narrative, but rather to reply to this narrative and to re-make its storytelling capacity. Their apparent fragmentation and rupture and their employment of the self-conscious and ironic are precisely what allows them to interrogate the politics and "justice" inherent within traditional narrative and to move toward some more equitable dialogue. That this movement is always in process, and not complete, is assumed. The textual purpose of frontier fiction is not revisionist in the purist sense of the word; instead these fictions struggle to always be in the process of revising, to always be in "dialectics" and never in the "episteme" (Lyotard 27).

The texts in *Coyote Kills John Wayne* do not simply offer another west; instead they challenge the reader to engage in the process of continuously remaking the West(s) and to engage in narrative gaming. Inevitably, this heightened attention to remaking and making narrative leads to questions concerning history—not just the history of the frontier, but history in general. What constitutes history? What are the range of practices that give one history legitimacy over another? How does the voice of the Other contend with the monolingual texts of so much of western history?

As fictions, the texts in this assemblage indeed challenge the very notion of history, suggesting through a range of strategies of representation, that history is but another fiction, "an art of memory made up of the thousand and one ways of composing a simulacrum with relics" (de Certeau 139). In particular, the American frontier is revealed as a kind of haunted site, a domain marked by absence. In this way, the texts often give voice to an alternate history, and indirectly expose the dynamics of a historical memory predicated on forgetting. The Other—the unrepresented, the invisible, the silenced, the marginalized of history—thus inevitably finds a presence in these alternative narratives. In this sense, these texts mark a return, what Michel de Certeau describes as the "haunting of history." As de Certeau reminds us, history is "founded on what it eliminates: it produces a "residue" condemned to be forgotten. But what was excluded reinfiltrates the place of its origin. . . . It resurfaces, it troubles, it turns the . . . feeling of being "at home" into an illusion, it lurks—this "wild," this "ob-scene" (4).

The haunting by alternative voices in *Coyote Kills John Wayne* raises important questions in regard to multiculturalism and postmodern aesthetics. Implicit in my presentation of these various postmodern voices is the argument that multicultural and postmodern(ism) need not be oppositional terms. Rather, postmodern—both as a problematic, as a strategy of representation, as a range of poststructuralist critical interventions— might be associated with an opening up and legitimation of a variety of narratives. It signals the collapse of the so-called *gran-récits* and master narratives, terms certainly attributable to traditional discovery and frontier narratives. While at times at odds with such Euro-American narratives as Freudian and Lacanian psychoanalytics, post-Marxist interpretive paradigms, and Derridean deconstruction, multiculturalism nonetheless has depended upon the dislocations of poststructuralism, and the attack on the primacy of "truth" and "transcendental signifiers." These truth effects have always played a part in disenfranchising and resisting Other voices. As some of the selections in *Coyote Kills John Wayne* demonstrate, considerable resonances can be developed between poststructuralist and postmodern theoretical interventions, and multicultural texts.

Within the context of postmodernism, these intertextual influences can be explained, not only by early postmodernist critical approaches that decentered Enlightenment paradigms, but by the (re)appropriation of such critical perspectives by critics and artists from a variety of cultures, including African American, Native American, Chicana/o, feminist and gay included. John Carlos Rowe has identified this shift by theorizing how postmodern critical advances have influenced a "postmodern politics," which informs many multicultural works such as those represented in *Coyote Kills John Wayne*. For Rowe, the often patriarchal and sexist fictions associated with high-postmodernism (emergent during the 1960s, '70s and '80s)— and with them, their penchant for formalism and ethereal experimentation—have to some degree given way to a postmodern, multicultural textual practice that "conceives of resistance and social reform as dependent on a critique of representation" (*Redrawing* 198). This emergent, postmodern *and* multicultural work thus often resists the over-aestheticized concerns often associated with avant-gardism, regrounding postmodernism as politically oppositional.

In *Narrative Chance*, Gerald Vizenor also underscores this theoretical relationship. He identifies within postmodernism the emergence of a resonant conceptual vocabulary capable of elucidating Native American trickster narratives. Vizenor aligns postmodernism with a concern for "normative discourse, authors, readers, trickster and comic world views rather than tragic themes, individualism and modernism" (4). Vizenor cites Lyotard's description of postmodernism in his assertion that it opens the way for alternative narratives: "The state of our culture following the transformations, which, since the end of the nineteenth century, have altered the game rules for science, literature and the arts." Asserts Vizenor, Lyotard's studies "place these transformations in the context of the crisis of narratives," and allude to the way postmodernist perspectives provide new ways of talking about Native American literature and tribal culture" (3-4). Concludes Vizenor, "The word *postmodernism* is a clever condition: an invitation to narrative chance in a new language game and an overture to amend the formal interpretation of tribal narratives." (4) Vizenor's comments might well be extended to include other marginalized voices that find resonance within postmodern perspectives. From this vantage, rather than looking at the ways in which postmodernism silences or elides the often marginalized perspectives inherent in alternative frontiers, *Coyote Kills John Wayne* strives to map points of convergence in their mutually informing vocabularies.

Clearly, a crucial point of convergence concerns questions about transcultural identities and their relationship to the historic construction of the frontier. Like their interrogation of history, these texts all ultimately confront questions concerning "mixed" identities, and the way in which frontier and discovery narratives have proven essential in projecting differences and providing a conceptual paradigm to mark Others. Historian Peter Shalin has asserted that frontiers represent "neither an 'interest' nor an 'ideology' but a belief that gave shape to an imagined space, bounded and unified" (1425).[9] But the space "bounded and unified" required internal policing, and to a large degree the conceptual apparatus that structured the "howling wilderness" and "wild frontier" has become internalized, a crucial conceptual boundary for enforcing difference and marginal identities amid a historic colonial landscape marked by cultural confrontations. Years before Turner's speech, in which the "imaginative" or "psychic" frontier was supplanting the "actual" frontier," so seemingly a progressive writer as James Fenimore Cooper was identifying cultural differences as essentially "internal." Cooper saw them as the products of an inward frontier that finally separated individuals by their "gifts" and by the indelible attributes of blood, which reflected ultimate differences among transcultural groups.

So, too, these fictions deal with the problems and opportunities resulting from the nomadic histories of oppressed peoples. From this juncture a variety of questions follow: What does it mean to live between cultures? To not have a homeland? What does it mean when the West is not west, or the frontier is not a frontier, but simply your land? Louise Erdrich has said that her fiction deals with the problem of "Who am I from?,"[10] suggesting that her fiction not only concerns identity, but how to live within certain identities, to exist in multiple cultures. In many ways, this is the central question posed by the "postmodern politics" of the texts assembled in *Coyote Kills John Wayne*. They remind us once again that the shifting boundaries and dusty topography defining the west and the frontier remain powerful markers within the social and political imaginary that defines us all.

New Frontiers: The Textual Concerns of Coyote Kills John Wayne

Coyote Kills John Wayne begins with "Arctic Revelations: William T. Vollmann's The Rifles and the Real of (Self)Discovery." The Rifles, William Vollmann's complicated and problematic installment is a part of his massive Seven Dreams project in which he describes the symbolic history of European and indigenous contact in the colonial conquest of the New World. Transhistorical in scope, Vollmann's fictions confront a number of important historical interventions by Europeans, including the first contact by Norse settlers with the Inuit of Icelandic regions, the French Jesuit and Iroquois wars, the British explorer John Franklin with the Inuits of the North Polar region.

From this perspective, Vollmann's narrative can best be understood as displaying the problematics of discovery as emergent within the postmodern frame. Vollmann's attempt to explore the historic contact between cultures is made emblematic at various historic junctures and unfolds as a highly self-conscious, self-reflexive, and resolutely conflicted examination of postcolonial problematics of representation. As evidenced in his imaginative merge between confessional, historic fantasy, metafictional inquiry, a crucial problem haunts his narrative. How does a desire to represent oneself against the Other—a desire emblematic in the literature of discovery and the frontier by Euro-explorers and settlers—haunt any attempt to know or confront Others? Through this confrontation with the "Real," Vollmann's text thus confronts and displays the impossibility of its own design, and it alludes to the frontier's force in cognitive mapping within colonial encounters.

"Dancing With the Dead: Ghost Dancing and Leslie Marmon Silko's *Almanac of the Dead*" explores how Silko's massive, encyclopedic narrative employs the historic politico-religious trope of ghost dancing to construct a counter-history of the conquest of the Americas. Ghost dancing emerged as a "new" religion, when the Paiute prophet Wovoka envisioned it in the 1870s, and spread to a number of Plains Indian tribes, where it eventually played a part in the Wounded Knee massacre of 1890. As detailed in Black Elk's account of his own experiences, ghost dancing allowed dancers access to the Indian dead and promised a future when land would be restored, the buffalo returned, and the living would be joined with the dead. Silko's account manipulates this counter-vision of the frontier, and thematically explores its apocalyptic and regenerative potential. Ghost dancing asserts presence for those who are absent; it reminds us that the structure of the frontier is predicated on violence and the resistance/confrontation with difference. As such, it has much in common with Jacques Derrida's notion of "hauntology," which marks an attempt to theorize how the marginalized returns, asserting itself within the structure of memory and hegemonic systems. Silko's fantasy counters European visions associated with the frontier; indeed, her text haunts such projections while asserting its own claims to the actual and conceptual topologies of the West.

Similarly combining Native American traditions with a "postmodern politics" concerned with representational systems, Thomas King's *Green Grass, Running Water* provides a compelling alternative way of reading "frontier history" and development. Abounding with intertextual references, puns, word games, and myriad literary and cultural allusions, *Green Grass* manages to merge postmodern aesthetics with Blackfoot traditions. "Coyote, Contingency, and Community: Thomas King's *Green Grass, Running Water* and Postmodern Trickster" explores how *Green Grass* represents a version of "postmodern trickster." As Gerald Vizenor reminds us, traditional Native American tricksters have always been subversive and, in many ways, preoccupied with representation and ways of seeing the world. "Postmodern tricksters" thus mark the remaking of traditional sacred trickster stories, within the contemporary context, and provide a way of resisting traditional categories associated with colonial domination of the frontier. Here, trickster counters traditional Eurocentric epistemologies inherent in the colonial constructions of the frontier and the west, and offers new ways of seeing. Ultimately, postmodern trickster Coyote offers a radical politics that functions on a number of levels.

"Displaced Horizons: Sergio Leone's Man With No Name; Films and the Politics of Postmodern Representation" examines Sergio Leone's spaghetti westerns and his antihero Clint Eastwood, who came to (em)body the postmodern condition. Sergio Leone once remarked that "when I look at John Wayne I see everything. When I look at Clint Eastwood I see nothing." Eastwood's face reflects the blank map of postmodernism. Indeed, Leone's West is overtly postmodern, a mélange of cartoon imagery, violence, and seemingly incoherent plot lines. But a closer examination reveals that Leone's version of the West plays with the very idea of the frontier territory in order to comment on its ideological force in American culture. Looked at from this perspective, Leone's vision emerges not so much as a representation of the "true West," but rather as a discursive field conditioned by cultural forces. "The Man With No Name" series came to theaters during the Cold War, and extended into the Vietnam era. "Displaced Horizons" argues that Leone's films self-consciously comment on the cultural moment of their origin, and simultaneously critique the way in which pop-culture westerns have functioned as vehicles for an imperialist ideology. Indeed, Leone's westerns point in spectacular fashion to the way in which the West has always to a large degree been a historical construction, mediated by colonial concerns, and a violent response to difference.

"Disruptive Genealogies: Louise Erdrich's *The Bingo Palace* and Native American Identities" elucidates an alternative definition of family and community. In the process, *The Bingo Palace* critiques the notion of "blood" lines and its relation to property and colonial codes of legitimacy. The fictive series unfolds on the Turtle Mountain Reservation as the Chippewa community must confront a range of colonial pressures, including the Dawes Act (1887). At the center of Erdrich's book is the question of identity. She ponders how to develop an identity-politics that can resist metaphors associated with origins and blood. In a discussion of mimicry and the performative aspects often exhibited by marginalized texts that operate from the "Third Space," postcolonial critic Homi Bhabha provides an important interpretive lens through which to read Erdrich's Turtle Mountain series of novels. Through their "genealogical structure," the novels seem to demand readers trace lineage and verify identities. But Bhabha allows us to see that Erdrich's schema comprises a ruse. As a kind of mimic text, *The Bingo Palace* actually only pretends to assert genealogical "roots." Ultimately, *The Bingo Palace* asks us to reconceptualize what constitutes "community" and "identity," and to map new possibilities for the frontier.

Finally, "In the Shadows of the Crazies: The Omnipresent Father and Thomas McGuane's Deadrock Novels" investigates the comic territory of McGuane's fictional Montana town of Deadrock. Though McGuane's fiction doesn't seem overtly postmodern in presentation, his highly ironized view of masculinity and its relation to western mythos represents a significant critique of Turner's rugged individualism. Operating within the tradition of Wister, Grey, and Hemingway, McGuane's Deadrock novels chart the relationship between traditional representations of the West and, at the same time, distance the reader from this tradition. As a Montana novelist (and avid sportsman), McGuane, in particular, presents a dysfunctional picture of Montana, an emblematic site where a "man's got to do what a man's got to do." Often, women and minorities suffer in McGuane's West, but they finally prevail by outwitting and beguiling Deadrock men. Deadrock comes to represent the perverse dark side of what Richard Slotkin has called the "gunfighter nation" that is America. McGuane's heroes are revealed as victims of masculine representations of the West, and their only hope for recovery is to accept a re-created West on different terms.

(Re)envisioning Frontiers

The effort to map the frontier space is not limited to contemporary authors. Visitors to the World's Columbian Exposition of 1893 were provided with a map of the "discovered" American world and its varied frontiers. Writes Richard Slotkin in his description of the Exposition:

Those who followed the paths prefigured in the Exposition's map and program were engaged by symbols, displays, and rituals that visualized the rapid course of American progress. The center-piece of the Exposition and the culmination of the typical itinerary was the "White City," an architectural extravaganza in ersatz marble representing the pinnacle of Euro-American civilization, the original "alabaster city.". . . The main road . . . lay through the Midway Plaisance . . . and "villages" displaying the wares and folkways of other nations, ethnological displays superintended by Franz Boas of the Smithsonian Institute, cheek by jowl with sideshows of the "Wild Man from Borneo" variety. The antipode of the White City was Buffalo Bill's Wild West. (Slotkin 63)

The exposition sought to contain the American expansionist mythology and to carefully map its course. It defined the spaces of the West and contained them within European history.

But even at this moment slippage occurred. Seemingly silent, the unincorporated narratives of African Americans, Native Americans, Asian Americans, and women undermined the cultural map. Other stories, narratives, and histories circulated. The postmodern moment is occupied with a similar pursuit as it "remaps" the contemporary world. The "cognitive mapping" undertaken by Jameson seeks to explore the ruptures inherent in late twentieth-century epistemology. But the map shifts and deconstructs. Other sites and other voices make the cartographer's task one of continued revision. In the end, there are only stories, fragments floating and remaking the territories, deserted towns and *ranchos* of the unknowable and thus unrepresentable region of that mythic space called the frontier.

Notes

1. See Richard Slotkin's *Gunfighter Nation: The Myth of the Frontier in Twentieth-century America* (New York: Harper Perennial, 1992). Slotkin identifies in Cody's show an emergent pop culture in which politics and spectacle merge to help foster a myth of the nation. Writes Slotkin: the function of realistic presentation is first to memorialize the real past as a "living monument," preserving not only the details of past heroism but also the moral truth that such a "bold dash" can only arise "from brave and noble inspiration." Having memorialized true history, the Wild West's next task is to translate history into useful instruction (82).

2. Regarding Cody's Wild West Show, see also Leslie Fiedler's *Buffalo Bill and the Wild West* (Pittsburgh: University of Pittsburgh Press, 1981), Walter Havighurst's *Buffalo Bill's Great Wild West Show* (New York: Random House, 1957), and Nelly Yost's *Buffalo Bill: His Family, Friends, Fame, Failures and Fortunes* (Chicago: Swallow Press, 1979).

3. See Philip Fisher's *Hard Facts* (New York: Columbia University Press, 1985).

4. This genealogical legacy is explored by Henry Nash Smith in his *Virgin Land: The American West as Symbol and Myth* (New York: Vintage Books, 1950). Smith notes how the dime novelists following Cooper used interchangeable "savages"—Indians, Mexicans, mestizos—depending on the historical context of the story. As such, Cooper's savages provided an archetype for the frontier Other.

5. Movies include *Silverado*, *Dances with Wolves*, and *The Young Riders*. Celebrities include Clint Black, Dwight Yokum, and, of course, Ronald Reagan—to name but a few.

6. Interestingly, Ihab Hassan's essay, "POSTmodernISM: A Paracritical Bibliography," was published in 1971 and a number of cultural critics read this moment as the instant when postmodernism's "pedigree" was established. See Charles Jencks, *Postmodernism* (New York: Rizzoli, 1987) and Ihab Hassan's *Paracriticism: Seven Speculations on the Times* (Urbana: University of Illinois Press, 1985).

7. See Alexis de Tocqueville's *Democracy in America* (1835).

8. See Fredric Jameson's "Cognitive Mapping," in Cary Nelson and Lawrence Grossberg's *Marxism and Interpretation of Culture* (Urbana: University of Illinois Press, 1979), 347–57.

9. This quote by French historian Peter Shalin's from his "Natural Frontiers Revisited: France's Boundaries since the Seventeenth Century" (*American Historical Review* 95, 1995) also appears in Stephen Greenblatt and Gile Gunn's provocative introduction to *Redrawing the Boundaries: The Transformation of English and American Literary Studies* (New York: MLA, 1992). In fact Greenblatt and Gunn develop the notion of shifting disciplinary frontiers to describe the current unstable terrain of English studies. Borders and frontiers are their central trope. Write Greenblatt and Gunn: "In general, we might think of the ways in which the frontiers are places of highest tension, vigilance, delay. But we should add that all talk of boundaries sits in a complex relation to a recognition of the larger whole within which most of the profession operates. We do not generally identify ourselves as occupying only one of the subgroups with which our volume is concerned. Each of those subgroups functions in a coordinated, if not exactly an integrated, system in which we may occupy more than one position. Within this system there are tensions, but these tensions are themselves part of the way the larger whole functions. The frontiers in our profession seem to exist only to be endlessly crossed, violated, renegotiated" (7).

10. See Joseph Bruchac's "Whatever Is Really Yours: An Interview with Louise Erdrich," in *Survival This Way: Interviews with American Indian Poets* (Tucson: University of Arizona Press, 1987).

Works Cited

Andalzua, Gloria. *Borderlands La Frontera: The New Mestiza*. San Francisco: Aunt Lute Books, 1987.

Cooper, James Fenimore. *Deerslayer*. New York: Penguin, 1980.

de Certeau, Michel. *Heterologies: Discourse on the Other*. Minneapolis: University of Minnesota Press, 1986.

Eichstaedt, Peter H. *If You Poison Us: Uranium and Native Americans*. Santa Fe: Red Crane Books, 1994.

Eisenman, Peter. *House of Cards*. New York: Oxford University Press, 1987.

Hall, Katherine. "Histories, Empires and the Post-Colonial Moment," in *The Post-Colonial Question: Common Skies Divided Horizon*, eds. Iain Chambers and Lidia Curti. London: Routledge, 1996.

Hutcheon, Linda. "Beginning to Theorize Postmodernism," in *A Postmodern Reader*. Albany: State University of New York Press, 1993.

Jameson, Fredric. "Cognitive Mapping," in *Marxism and Interpretation of Culture*, eds. Cary Nelson and Lawrence Grossberg. Urbana: University of Illinois Press, 1983.

———. *Postmodernism, Or, The Cultural Logic of Late Capitalism*. Durham, N.C.: Duke University Press, 1991.

Lyotard, Jean-François. *Just Gaming*, with Jean-Loup Thebaud, trans. by Wlad Godzich. Minneapolis: University of Minnesota Press, 1979.

McHale, Brian. *Constructing Postmodernism*. London: Routledge, 1992.

Mourning Dove. *Cogewa, the Half-Blood: A Depiction of the Great Montana Cattle Range*. Lincoln: University of Nebraska Press, 1981.

Owens, Louis. *Other Destinies: Understanding the American Indian Novel*. Norman: University of Oklahoma Press, 1992.

Silko, Leslie Marmon. "Private Property," in *New Worlds of Literature: Writing from America's Many Cultures*, eds. Jerome Beaty and Paul Hunter. New York: W.W. Norton, 1989.

Slotkin, Richard. Gunfighter Nation: *The Myth of the Frontier in Twentieth-Century America*. New York: Harper Perennial, 1993.

Tafuri, Manfredo. *The Sphere and the Labyrinth: Avant-gardes and Architecture from Piranesi to the 1970's*. Cambridge: MIT Press, 1987.

Turner, Frederick Jackson. *The Significance of the Frontier in American History*. Norman: University of Oklahoma Press, 1963.

Vizenor, Gerald. *Narrative Chance*. Albuquerque: University of New Mexico Press, 1989.

CHAPTER TWO

Arctic Revelations: William T. Vollmann's *The Rifles* and the Real of (Self) Discovery

> Power resides in the capacity to advance into emptyness. All that gives us the figures of the apparatus of domain in which the revelation of another reveals itself (*s'aveve*) as adventure.
>
> —Jacques Lacan, *Seminar VII*

> He could see the sutures in its white skull. It was not featureless, but pocked and drifted here and there, runneled and cracked—but mainly it was featureless, like one of those Nasa photos of the moon.
>
> —William T. Vollmann, *The Rifles*

(Ice)olations and Self-Reflections

TOWARD THE BEGINNING of *The Rifles* (1994), the third volume of his visionary *Seven Dream* series, William T. Vollmann—or perhaps more accurately, the textual "Vollmann" (a.k.a. John, John Franklin, Captain Subzero, William the Blind, "he," "you," and "me")—makes a curious discovery in the refractive surface of the Arctic seashore. Imbedded in the natural iconography of the dazzling fissures and ice forms is the coded message that Vollmann\Subzero shares a haunting affinity with Sir John Franklin, the doomed nineteenth-century Arctic explorer at the center of *The Rifles*, who spent a lifetime attempting to forge a Northwest passage. Gazing at the words formed in the gelid landscape, Vollmann explains:

[t]hese characters which he now saw were much more definite than the faces one half-sees in clouds. He believed in them. . . . [I]n the ice-shadow, he wrote out the transliterations with his fingers:

ja n va ra ng ka li n

Yawn Varangkalean.

Yon Vranklin.

John Franklin.

* * *

The ice-orthography was not perfect, of course. . . . [C]orruptions were expected—so Franklin was his twin. (48)

For readers of Vollmann's previous Dream novels—*The Ice Shirts* (1990) and *Fathers and Crows* (1992)—the moment characteristically displays the author's combination of erudition and mysticism. Beyond this, however, the strange merge between Vollmann and his historical subject provides an emblematic juncture from which to explore how *The Rifles* represents a significant development in Vollmann's Seven Dreams project.

Among postmodernists contending with the problematics of the colonial frontier, or what Louise Pratt calls the "contact zone"—and with it, the familiar tropes often associated with "native encounters"—Vollmann's Seven Dreams series occupies a unique and curious position.[1] Vollmann himself has described his massive narrative project as an attempt to write "symbolic history" (*Frequency*) of the European colonial conquests of the indigenous populations of North America. An audacious combination of confessional, genealogical, fantastic, historical meditation, each of Vollmann's transhistorical novels emerge as complex interrogations of a variety of historically resonant "intrusions" by European explorers. *The Ice Shirts*, the first in the series, maps the violent collision of cultures embodied in the tenth-century Norse conquest of the Icelandic regions of North America. *Father and Crows* concerns the eighteenth- and nineteenth-century religious wars between the Colonial French Jesuits and the Iroquois. *The Rifles* explores the British explorer John Franklin's attempt to chart passage over the North Pole, and its devastating and complex legacy.[2]

What makes Vollmann's project curious, however, is not so much the historical occasions that structure his narratives, but rather the degree to which Vollmann himself enters into the texts. As his recondite appendices reveal in *The Rifles*, Vollmann's entrance into the nightmarish and hallucinogenic narrative actually occurred. While pursuing his *Sixth Dream*, Vollmann actually *did* traverse Canada and Greenland to spend time amid the gelid environs of Resolute Bay. Vollmann *did* survive twelve nights in a barren North Pole ice station where he nearly froze to death amid the Arctic desolation. And, significantly, Vollmann *did* develop numerous interpersonal relationships with various Inuits, whose "lived experience" and own stories prove central to Vollmann's representation of Sir John Franklin's attempt to map a northern passage, and its ultimate legacy of devastation to Inuit cultures.[3]

Indeed, while critical attention to biography often proves extraneous, in the context of Vollmann's professed desire to write a "symbolic history" of European colonial interventions, it illuminates a central thematic focus of *The Rifles* (and beyond, the entire Dream novels): Vollmann's problematic and unending encounter with himself. As his own "real-life" travels amid the colonial frontiers attempt to reveal, Vollmann seems compelled by a desire to escape the mediatory realms of representation that haunt ethnographic representations of the Other. But as the ice inscribed merge between Sir John Franklin and "Vollmann" suggests, Vollmann's narrative ultimately stages the impossibility of representing the Other. From this perspective, Vollmann's *The Rifles* proves resonant when read through Jacques Lacan's famous configuration of the Subject and the Other within the triadic realm of the Imaginary, the Symbolic, and the Real. Moreover, *The Rifles* can be understood as an attempt to get beyond the Imaginary and the Symbolic, moving toward the elusive Real.

Ultimately, however, in spite of its desire to encounter and "know" the Other, Vollmann's narrative instead allegorizes its own failures, reveals the limitations of its own horizon. Beyond, in its deliberate blurring and deconstruction of traditionally fixed categories (fiction\biography, history\memory, reality\construction), *The Rifles* reveals the ways in which these categories of perception—like the Other—cannot escape the ruthless logic of the Subject. But in order to understand how *The Rifles* represents a move toward the Real, and provides a gloss on the entire *Seven Dreams* project, it is necessary first to briefly return to Lacan's familiar description of the emergence of the Subject within the subject-forming matrix of the Imaginary, the Symbolic, and the Real.

Toward the Real

For Lacan, the initial glimmers of subjectivity—of an emerging Self—begin within the realm of the Imaginary, which he associates with a child's recognition of his/her own image in the mirror. In this preverbal setting, the specular image refracted back to the subject presents both Otherness, and intimations of the Self. The mirror stage thus inaugurates a divided Self, a Self haunted by its own incompleteness. Without words or semiotic constructs that will help regulate the Self, the emergent subject is "able to sense Otherness in its own specular image but unable to articulate and thereby stabilize that difference . . . ; it finds itself both narcissistically attached to that image and antagonistically contesting its position" (Palumbo-Liu 78).

Within the Symbolic, the second term in Lacan's triadic paradigm, the subject enters the realm of language, in which meaning and conceptions of a Self contend with the deferral and absence that haunts the subject. Here, subjectivity undergoes a continual process of self-maintenance. Language and discursivity function to maintain the "fiction" of a unified Self. Predicated on the law, the Symbolic orders the world, maintaining the subject. Significantly, for Lacan, the Symbolic precedes the Self, always already refracted in the structure of language and signification itself, which functions through deferral and absence. This prefiguring aspect of the Symbolic and its relation to language inheres in Lacan's famous phrase: "The unconscious is structured like a language." Indeed, the Symbolic "dominates and legislates the spaces open to the subject, allowing only certain kinds of signification and repressing or distorting others" (78).

Given this prefiguring capacity of the Imaginary and Symbolic to subsume Others, Lacan's model of subjectivity obviously has profound implications regarding western discourses of discovery and "the native encounter," in which the exploring subject seeks not only new horizons, but Others, who will ultimately be bound within the explorer's unfolding psychic drama. Exploration narratives constantly reveal this process in fantasy projections of the simultaneously exotic and feared native. Ethnographic writing, in turn, attempts to fix the Other, transforming the native into artifacts (objects) in the service of the exploring subject. This process, to a large extent, defines the western mode of colonization—discourse eventually replaces the material violence, capturing the Other in narratives of conquest, domination, rehabilitation.

In discussing the subject's drive to reinscribe the Other within the context of its own spectral processes of self-making, Lacan tellingly refers to the process as "discovery":

Power resides in the capacity to advance into emptiness. All of that gives us the figures of the apparatus of a domain in which revelation of another reveals itself (s'aveve) as adventure. The meaning of the word recognition tends towards that which it assumes in every exploration, with all the accents of militancy and nostalgia we can invest in it. ("Camp" 146–73)

For Lacan, discovery represents an intertwined, intersubjective process of self-discovery and self-deception. The revelation of the Other is consumed, finally, by the fantasy of the Self. Kim Michasiw describes this interior process: "Any exploration of objects is an attempt to re-find. The quest is always for the lost which may be re-cognized. . . . Lacan's power of recognition is a self-authentication through a fiction of going boldly into the void—supposedly of the Other but entirely prescripted by the subject" (155).

In mapping colonialist literature against Lacan's model, Abdul JanMohamed identifies two forms of colonial literature—that structured by the Symbolic and that by the Imaginary. For JanMohamed, Imaginary colonialist literature projects a binary universe in which the Eurocentric colonizer interpolates the native as a fantasm in the service of the self. JanMohamed refers to this interpolative process as the "manichean allegory." Imaginary colonial texts reveal no self-consciousness about their dependence on the manichean allegory for structure, meaning, and textual identifications. Symbolic texts, suggests JanMohammed, self-consciously and "self-reflexively" engage the problematic of the Imaginary, but nonetheless risk reinscribing the Other within the familiar field of binary oppositions. These two forms of colonialist literature connect Joseph Conrad's *Heart of Darkness* and E. M. Forster's *A Passage to India* to Isak Dinesen's *Out of Africa* and Nadine Gordimer's *July's People*. Each of these texts, in their own way, represent a kind of continuum, in which the mirror stage and Symbolic order structure narratives in which first worlders confront inhabitants of the third world.

Significantly, according to JanMohamed, through self-reflexive rupturing of the binaries that structure its relationships, certain Symbolic texts have the potential to destabalize the "libidinal economy of the 'imaginary'" (85). For JanMohamed, such colonial texts resist seeking a "syncretic solution to the manichean opposition of the colonizer and the colonized" (85); rather, they "realize that syncretism is impossible within the power relations of colonial society because such a context traps the writer in the libidinal economy of the 'imaginary.'" Thus, by "[b]ecoming reflexive about its context, by confining itself to a rigorous examination of the 'imaginary' mechanisms of colonialist mentality, this type of fiction manages to free itself from the manichean allegory" (85).

JanMohamed's assertion, however, raises an important question with regard to the colonial context of writing. If, as Lacan's paradigm suggests, the Self is in a sense always at conflict with its own "fiction"—its own impossibility, or limit—then how can we imagine that the colonial context (first

worlders writing about third worlders) can escape the dialectical and refractive feature of its ultimate self-serving aspect and the haunting alienation that marks the Imaginary? JanMohamed's insistence on the liberative
potential of Symbolic texts thus risks underrepresenting the fundamental
determinative structure of discovery narratives and their primary relationship to a "political unconscious" whose cognitive topology they mirror. Indeed, if as Lacan reminds us, "every desire is at base a desire to impose oneself on another and to be recognized by the Other," then narratives of the
encounter ultimately are self-serving in the extreme, consonant with material domination and violence visited on native peoples.

Of course, a third term remains in Lacan's famous model, the Real,
which evades JanMohamed's analysis but, I would argue, proves resonant
when discussing *The Rifles* and Vollmann's entire Dreams project. The Real
is that which lies beyond the subject-forming mechanisms of the Imaginary
and the Symbolic, that "absolute Otherness" that lies beyond the "wall of
language" (Žižek: *Everything* 245). As such, the Real identifies the aleatory
spaces in the subject, which can be sensed, but which defy recognition: "the
ineliminable residue of all articulation, the foreclosed element, which may
be approached, but never grasped" (*Four* 280). In *Looking Awry*, Slavoj
Žižek identifies this void as "the subject beyond subjectivity," the nonhisto-
rizable and "unrepresentable" site that Lacan claims to be "the 'hard-
kernel' around which every symbolization fails" (33–35).[4]

In *The Rifles* Vollmann arrives at a similar destination—what might be
called the Real of ethnographic representations. Though Vollmann's postmodern narrative interrogates a range of "knowledges" that depend on and
are structured through the Other, it ultimately confronts the "lack" or
"nonhistoricizable site" that haunts the subject, and correspondingly all attempts to represent the Other. Through this staging of the "impossibility"
of the Self, traced by Vollmann's ultimate indeterminacy within the text
and marked by the "recognition" of his own "decenteredness" within the
ice forms, *The Rifles* thus reinscribes the entire Seven Dreams enterprise
within a hermeneutics of the Real. From this perspective, Vollmann's implicit desire to move beyond the "libidinal economies" of the Symbolic,
signaled by his own "real-life" entrance into his narratives, his own "real-
life encounters with Others, must fail. This recognition, this movement toward the Real, haunts all of his "symbolic histories."

If Linda Hutcheon has identified postmodern fiction concerned with
historicity and the problematic of representing the past as "historiographic
metafiction," then Vollmann's *The Rifles* might be called "ethnographic

metafiction." As such it obsesses on the formation of the explorer\subject, constantly deconstructs itself to the point of the beyond, which, like the Arctic landscape, consumes all in its void. Vollmann's psychic slippage—Vollmann the "real" person, "Vollmann the narrator," Vollmann the lover, Vollmann the Arctic explorer, Vollmann the time tourist, Vollmann the Other—ultimately signals this void, this problematic that structures encounter narratives, and which Vollmann's own narrative project cannot evade. Here, the transcultural and transhistorical colonial frontiers Vollmann attempts to explore turn back on themselves, return always to the cul-de-sac of the Self and its violent appropriation of Others.

As in his other Dream novels, the meditative narrative of *The Rifles* centers on a historical instance of colonial contact—the British explorer Sir John Franklin's doomed expeditions to the North Pole. Commissioned in 1845 to return for a fourth time to the Pole, Franklin's final trip fails horribly when his ship becomes ice bound. On his voyages, Franklin intruded on the lives of the Inuit in a variety of ways, but perhaps no more so than by introducing the repeating rifle to their culture. Vollmann associates the introduction of the repeating rifle with a shift in Inuit lifestyle that ultimately proves disastrous. For Vollmann, the advanced armament, like the iron axe in the *Ice Shirts* and the arquebus in *Fathers and Sons*, clearly becomes a material and technological emblem of the ideological violence visited on the indigenous by the European colonial invaders. The historic, material introduction of rifles thus becomes emblematic of the discursive violence implicit in Franklin's own detailed discursive accounts of his mission, which, like other discovery narratives, ideologically function around encountering the Other.

In *The Rifles*, as in his other Dream Novels, Vollmann's inquiry into the events that lead to Franklin's icy fate, represents a journey into the past and a journey into the present. In his alternately humorous and recondite appendices, Vollmann explains that he conducted exhaustive historical research in the process of writing his "Dream," including interrogating Franklin's exploration journals, and that, like Franklin, he traveled to absolute north. Readers confronting this at the textual level thus encounter a strange, postmodern mélange of genres—confessional, metahistory, discovery narrative, diary, and novelistic fiction. Throughout however, Vollmann persistently returns to the idea that as a narrator, as an explorer, as a historian, he cannot escape himself. Everywhere, in the self-reflexive processes of both his physical and symbolic journeys, he is refracted back to himself.

In the Lacanian Imaginary, the *imago* emerges as the central trope, the miragelike image that is reflected back to the subject. Lacan presents the *imago* as a "form of the body" that "symbolizes the mental permanence of the I, at the same time as it prefigures its alienating destination . . . the statue in which man projects himself" *(Ecrits* 2). The *imago* as such is refractory, is both aleatory and "I," at once a "statue" of the Self and the embodiment of alienation. Carole-Ann Tyler elucidates:

> The subject can never reconcile the split between itself and its mirror imago, the eye which sees and the eye which is seen, the I who speaks and I who is spoken, the subject of desire and the subject of demand, who must pass through the defiles of the others as signifiers. It is this alienation, this gap between being and meaning, subject and signifier, self and other, which the classical realist system of representation would suture. (218)

The *imago*, then, becomes both a site of desire and a site of anxiety, a site always leading back to the "gaps" and "distances" within the fiction of the unified Self.

In *The Rifles* the experimentalist Vollmann obviously resists "realist" representations. But the refractive and Self-reflexive aspects of the *imago* and Imaginary haunt his narrative. Ice, with all its resonances—dangerous, seductive, pervasive, scary, and beautiful—is the central, overdetermining image that persists throughout the narrative. As Vollmann writes when first encountering the polar regions, "although this place of ship-shaped icebergs was a paradise of sorts, you suspected that other illusions and deceptions might beset you in this mirrorless house of mirrors" (3). Later vistas dissolve into "ice-shadows" and a place of "shine-doubles," where Vollmann's own image—*imago*—is constantly refracted back to him. Within this all-encompassing ice-scape, Vollmann's eyes indeed are "the eye which sees and the eye which is seen." Like Sir John Franklin, who struggles to free himself from this frozen landscape, Vollmann too, on a metaphoric level, struggles within the reflective realm of the Imaginary.

As Lacan reminds us, the Imaginary and *imago* are identified with primal alienation, the emergence of a split Self that will forever haunt the Self. Vollmann's shape-shifting and subject-sliding in the narrative reflect this alienation and decentered constitution. His identification with Franklin, on the textual level, blurs the boundaries of the Self. Readers must constantly search for a ground, a way to discover which narrative voice confronts them. Who is "speaking"—the historic Franklin or Subzero, who is Vollmann himself? What constitutes the past; the present? Moreover, confronting the panels that move back and forth temporally, between the present of Vollmann's searches and the past of Franklin's searches, becomes disorienting for the reader. Is this the past in terms of the present, as Foucault calls his genealogical inquiries; or is it the present in terms of the past?[5]

The Symbolic, predicated on language and the law,[6] ultimately stabilizes the refractive aspects of the Imaginary that inform Vollmann's refractive surfaces. Yet Vollmann's linguistic confusion performatively engages in a kind of Symbolic jouissance, disrupting the logic of the Symbolic. As David Palumbo-Liu notes, "Lacan's Symbolic order is largely made up of 'shifters,' especially personal pronouns. One gives up one's proper name in order to represent oneself as I" (79). In *The Rifles*, however, this "I" remains indeterminate, confused, and overdetermined by Vollmann's textual strategies. Vollmann's lexical confusion thus forces readers to confront the "libidinal" economies that structure both the Imaginary and the Symbolic. As such Vollmann himself exists not so much as a singular designation, but rather a conflicted point of enunciation evincing the realities of a decentered, non-Enlightenment subject. His murky identification with Franklin in the ice-forms signals this trajectory, which ultimately leads toward the Real of the encounter, which can only be hinted at in linguistic jouissance and verbal recognitions.

Beyond this, the conflation between the explorer Franklin and the writer Vollmann/Subzero, reveals a crucial problematic that lies at the center of colonial narratives. The narrator wants to describe new worlds, encounter alien vistas, and record the history of another race. He wants to escape the limitations of his own existence and see something else. But as his vision moves outward, his sight is obscured by his own reflection. Hence all "discovery" becomes fixed within the closed sphere of the Self. All exploration is self-exploration. Thus the merger with Franklin's ego provides no relief to Vollmann/Subzero; it merely illuminates his own transgressions and isolation.

Like the subject of the Lacanian paradigm, Vollmann in *The Rifles*—indeed, in his entire Dream series—is avowedly obsessed with that idea of the Other. But, unlike the Lacanian child, Vollmann is self-conscious knowing that we are all trapped by ourselves, unable to escape the refractory lenses of ego. His text probes the Other knowing it to be mere projection—an imaginary icon whose features appear uncannily tangible but is frozen forever beneath its ice sheath. He has lost belief in the idealized, in the conception of completion, and sees all as reflection of his own limitation. Thus, it is not that his narrative is informed with autobiography or that he desires self-knowledge in the most banal of ways. Rather, Vollmann acknowledges that the very categories in which selfhood is generally invested are shallow, and that the mirror eventually points back toward our own hideous deformities.

For the textual Vollmann/Sir John/Captain Subzero, the Other is embodied in his tragic lover Reepah, who dies in "the present" of the narrative (indeed, such distinctions between past and present dissolve for Vollmann) by suicide. As the different levels of the narrative develop, it becomes painfully clear that her inexorable doom is the result of two realities that are as interwoven as the strands of a double helix. First, she is a persecuted Inuit struggling to live under the tyranny of the Euro-American "civilizing" process, which Vollmann metaphorically relates to the introduction of the repeating rifle to Inuit culture. Second, she is trapped within Vollmann's narrative. In each case the result is tragically, inequitably the same—Reepah's eventual destruction. Moreover, the fact that Vollmann/Subzero loves her ultimately does little to alter her fate.

The problematic relationship between Vollmann (principally referred to as Subzero or John in these sections) and Reepah, which forms the parallel discourse to Franklin's narrative of discovery, becomes apparent almost immediately in *The Rifles*. When he returns to the icy Inukat, presumably to further research *The Rifles*, requiring him to endure twelve horrific nights in an abandoned meteoric station amid the ice wastes of the Northern Cross so as to better empathize/merge with Sir John Franklin, Vollmann anxiously questions the painful rekindling of his relationship to Reepah. Vollmann writes, "How can it ever work? It was courageous as he could be to see her at all, to kiss her. What if he stayed with her? Would he start to hate himself"? (62).

Vollmann's increasing self-consciousness about appropriation causes him to question his relationship with Reepah, who clearly develops as both an Inuit Other and intimate. Sleeping near her, he accedes to a "positive affirmations" suggestion card, which ironically notes: *Just for today I will respect my own and others' boundaries* (70). But in his journey to know her, as well as the Inuit past and present, Vollmann's overwhelming desire to be with Reepah necessarily leads him to violate her boundaries and collude in her erasure. In this context, Vollmann's consumptive passion self-consciously references a subjectivity centered in the Lacanian landscape of desire, in which Others are necessarily narcissistic projections of the Self. As Vollmann writes: "[H]e needed more than anything in the world to dissolve into her. . . . [A]lthough he had not yet penetrated her because that would be the literal incarnation of himself within her, a change of being; he would become her then, alien, lovely and loved" (75). Here, Vollmann cannot escape the seductions of a libidinal economy founded on the Other. Thus, although a profession of "love," his linguistic fantasy of merger inexorably marks the Self-serving component of the Western self-making process, and his acute awareness that his fascination with and attraction to the "exotic" Reepah represents a perverse involution of history carried out on a personal level. This realization forms the painful subtext of *The Rifles*. Like Sir John Franklin, whose ice-bound prison leads to unspeakable pain—metaphorically (dis)embodied in the image of cannibalism—Vollmann's experiences lead him to tortured questions concerning the all-consuming nature of his own narrative project. Reepah's death leads to the inevitable conclusion: inquiries into the Other are impossible; the pain such inquiries inflict is real and unescapable. Indeed, even Vollmann's postmodern ethnography cannot avoid this reality.

Absolute (Real) North

In *Looking Awry*, Slavoj Žižek associates the Lacanian Real, that non-historicizable site and absolute Otherness that lies beyond the "wall of language," with postmodernism itself. For Žižek, the Real is fleetingly apparent in the Lacanian "synthome," (symptom), which simultaneously has the power to haunt and give pleasure, and in the Freudian/Lacanian idea of *das Ding*, which leads back to the Real. The "synthome," like *das Ding* (the thing), thus intrudes, hinting at the unrepresentable, the void that haunts the Self and carries with it the recognition of the Self's impossibility and limits. For Žižek, the "synthome" and *das Ding* replace such modernist categories as metaphor, mimesis, and sign, and allude to the fiction of the "centered" Enlightenment Subject that cannot be maintained in the postmodern context. In the *The Sublime Object of Ideology*, Žižek writes: "[W]hat lies beyond is not the Symbolic order but a real kernel, a traumatic core. To designate it, Lacan uses a Freudian term: *das Ding*, the thing as incarnation of the impossible *jouissance* (the term Thing is to be taken here with all the connotation it possesses in the domain of horror science fiction)" (132). As a "grimace of the Real," the "synthome" and the *das Ding* thus come forth as exteriorized incarnations of the exterior void, the "embodiment" of the limited logic of the Self.

From this perspective, *The Rifles* and Vollmann's excursion toward the Other can be read as allegorizing this confrontation with the Real, as textualizing this recognition and postmodern epiphany. In this sense, *The Rifles* might best be approached as a kind of ontological performance, in which

Vollmann's physical journey cannot be separated from the text. Rather, the two are intertwined: the text as performance, his performance as text. In this way he approaches the Real of exploration narratives. His actual journey informs his textual journey.

At the epicenter of this performance is Vollmann's real-life travels to absolute north, during which he survived alone in an isolated weather station at absolute north. As detailed in the text, Vollmann's experience is excruciating; he nearly dies amid the Arctic wastes. That Insachsen will in some sense represent—as synthome—the Real (the Real of Vollmann's consumptive desire to encounter the Other, the Real of Reepah's pain, the Real of the place of the Other in the construction of the Self) becomes clear as Vollmann approaches the ice wastes that surround magnetic north, a place that "faces true nothingness" (253). In its barrenness and frigid bitterness, the place transforms into a monstrous vision—not unlike some improbable horror movie creature, at once featureless and animal-like. As "synthome," this vision of approaching absolute north proves sickening: "He could see the sutures in its flat white skull. It was not featureless, but pocked and drifted here and there, runneled and cracked—but *mainly* it was featureless, like one of those NASA photographs of the moon, because snow covered it; after only a moment the eye began to ache with failure to assign any scale; it was sickening. . . . He did not want to look" (263). And yet Vollmann proceeds, driven by a desire to consummate his encounter with the frozen wastes, to identify with Franklin.

At absolute north, Vollmann indeed undergoes extreme hardship. He thinks of Franklin, and of Reepah, to whom he fears he has been "evil." Isolated in an abandoned weather station, he soon begins to feel alienated and increasingly fearful. The frozen surroundings correspondingly become more menacing; sleep evades him. Significantly, he begins to disassociate from his own body. His hands and feet become "dead again" (277), and after time he can no longer feel his arms and legs.

The anesthetized feet are a reminder of John Franklin's consumed appendages and clearly become emblematic. Vollmann embraces pain and horror in an effort to break out of his self-contained isolation. But the numbness of his toes metaphorically signals his difficulty with emotion. In an effort to force feeling, the narrator(s) kisses his moribund hands. He takes a masochistic pleasure in doing so, because pain fills a double function of both punishing the self and heightening consciousness. Coldness here, as with the appendages, are "synthomes" in a "real sense," harbingers of *das Ding*.[7]

Here, both in "real-life" and textually, Vollmann confronts the Real. Mirroring colonial discovery texts, his text is revealed within this moment of the staging of Franklin's isolation as teleological and self-reflexive in many ways as disembodied as the Self. At this point, Vollmann's novel apprehends in his own *imago*—refracted in the dissociated body parts. In a real sense, Vollmann confronts absolute north: the colonial frontier has disappeared, metamorphosed into the directionless point at absolute center, where Vollmann resides, surrounded by whiteness and cold. If, as Lacan reminds us, every desire is at base a desire to possess the Other, then Vollmann's text displays that truth. As an ontological performance, the text arrives at this inescapable recognition—the recognition of the place that lies beyond subjectivity, beyond the "wall of language," the void that haunts all inquiries into knowing the Other.

But even these horrific passages—Franklin's and Vollmann's—fail to provide absolution, or an escape from "symbolic history." Vollmann's injuries end with his being frozen; he cannot feel himself and yet, ironically, this results in a heightened, more painful, self-awareness. It is his fate to be locked within himself, staring outward at the reflective ice. He is beneath the Northern Cross but there is no benediction and no new terrain.

As if to underscore this consumptive nature of the Real, *The Rifles*, curiously, closes with a "Morality Play in One Act," in which various displaced Inuits testify to the destructive effects of the current Canadian Inuit relocation programs. Taken from documented testimony, the "voices" in the play suggest Vollmann's sincere desire to allow the Inuits to speak for themselves. Revealed in the testimony is the painful reality of Canadian and U.S. oppression. As Samwillie Elijasialuk testifies: "I was one of the ones sent to Grise Fiord. When we landed there, we were put to work unloading drums and coal for the police. . . . [I]t caused me hurt. I now have no shame about telling how police used to say, 'You can trade only after I use your woman.' They used to do this, and I still hurt about it. There are so many wrongs (334)."

But while Vollmann's dialogical attempt to represent "true" Inuit voices proves compelling, Vollmann recognizes the impossibility that their voices can remain isolated from his own discursive structure, from his own point of view. *The Rifles* ends not with the Inuit voices, but with Vollmann's own:

. . . [F]ate is different before the barrel and behind the hammer, the hammer that falls so heavily upon the firing pin. . . . But I say to you who are strangers . . .—I say to you others: As you crouch there with stock against your shoulder, pray for the caribou. Pray that your shot is not true. (341)

Vollmann's *The Rifles* thus becomes, finally, a critique of Western epistemology, its incessant preoccupation with the self, and the violence that results. Lacan, Freud, Christianity, or self-help, or history—Vollmann suggests that all of it simply accentuates the "I" until it becomes all-encompassing. Psychoanalysis might argue that self-consciousness can be liberating, but Vollmann demonstrates that self-consciousness—seeing the Other and the mirror for what they are—simply intensifies the experience of selfhood. Our way of seeing, of perceiving, has become deathly. We kill both the subject—in this case the Inuit—and ourselves. Rather than constituting an act of confession, guilt becomes one more mode of masochistic wallowing in a self-created despair. There is no way out.

Desolation Station

If modernism was marked by its insistent "discovery" of the unconscious and consciousness itself, then postmodernism must be similarly defined by a kind of metaconsciousness and a sense that there is no differentiation between consciousness and the world. If the world itself is revealed in texts, then all forays into the world are in the end mere expeditions into ourselves. Vollmann's brilliance lies in his ability to articulate this condition—tortuously, terribly, and truly. We are all (at/with) Subzero. Our very interpretations of our/Subzero's state simply exacerbate it.

The destruction of the Inuit is our own, both our own fault and our own death. The mirror cracks as we look into it and read our own demise. Perhaps a way of reading Vollmann is to see *The Ice Shirts*, as Vollmann has maintained in an interview, as "the beginning of American history." *Fathers and Crows* continues this saga of exploitation and erasure through its exploration of the effects of Catholicism on the Inuit population. Emblematic of this process is the icon of the cross, which merges guilt, forgiveness, death, and erasure. Certainly we are implicated, but from a distance. But in *The Rifles*, it is our own history that is explored, with the Inuit functioning as a means to grapple with these hard issues. It is here that we learn that history is not remote but ever-present, and that it is at once both a mythology and one of the brutal facts of our own existence.

The problematics of history and historical representation necessarily impact narrative, argues Fredric Jameson. Even as literature struggles to interrogate, as well as represent the familiar, it undergoes a kind of "slippage" and a reconstruction through the prism of ideology. Historicism, contends Jameson, as well as literary representation of the historical, is always "dramatized by the peculiar, unavoidable, yet seemingly unresolvable alteration between Identity and Difference. . . . [W]e cannot opt for one or another of these possibilities" ("Marxism" 150). We are of necessity caught between being beckoned seductively by the Real and simultaneously being obscured and "managed" by the impulses of narrative. It is this terrain of quiet slippage, haunted by the omnipresence of the real, which Vollmann painfully explores.

Jameson writes in "The Cultural Logic of Late Capitalism": "If we are unable to unify the past, present, and future of the sentence, then we are similarly unable to unify the past, present, and future of our own biographical experience or psychic life. . . . In our present context, this experience suggests . . . a space of praxis; thereby isolated, that present engulfs the subject with indescribable vividness" (59–92).

The predicament outlined by Jameson finds resonance in Vollmann's novels, and suggests to what degree Vollmann's historical anxiety is emblematic of the entire project of postmodernity. We are of necessity at odds with our narrative, which must always "process" the Real. Jameson further asserts:

[I]f, however, we try to accustom ourselves to thinking of the narrative text as a process whereby something is done to the Real, whereby operations are performed on it and it is one way or another managed or indeed neutralized . . . then clearly we will have to begin to think of the Real as something outside the work, of which the latter stands as an image or makes a representation, but rather as something borne within and vehiculated by the text itself . . . interiorized . . . the raw material on which the textual operation must work. ("Of Islands" 81)[8]

In this respect, Vollmann's *Seven Dreams* texts offer a counter-narrative to an idea of a Self exteriorized, a Self that allows for a particular kind of historicism prevalent in Americanist studies. As Tom Cohen argues, Americanists have been prone to display a preoccupation with the materiality of history and "ideological demystification," rather "than of aesthetic disinvestment" (353), which a Lacanian model provides. In particular, Cohen attacks the familiar neopragmatist position of reclaiming history as a "sublime object," while neglecting the interiorized spaces of the Subject that haunts all representations and fantasy projections of the past and its relation to Others.

Invoking Žižek's readings of Lacan, Cohen suggests that neopragmaticism risks reinscribing an isolate "American self," evading the question of how the very construction of the Self provokes and influences a range of textual constructions of history. Writes Cohen:

What emerges is that . . . neopragmatism . . . represents a monumental regression within the name of the American agenda. If, as Žižek implies, a certain Americanism is manifest in postmodern popular culture . . . , it supersedes the domain of the Symbolic in a kind of psychotic or anti-Oedipal poetics. . . . If so, [neopragmatism] may represent the attempt to return to a defensive posture in this regard, inscribing themselves in an Americanist rhetoric of the self that is the classic evasion. (354)

As demonstrated, Vollmann's narrative cannot "evade" the Self, but rather unmasks the operations that inscribe its rhetorical construction. Moreover, it illuminates how such categories as "history," "frontier," and "discovery" reflect an interiorized libidinal economy that haunts colonial encounters.

For Vollmann, for the fictive SubZero, and for the reader, narrative engagement with the Seven Dream series involves acknowledgment that we stand at the base camp of this Arctic "textual operation." As readers we are compelled to acknowledge our own complicity and to read our own distinction from the Other and our disassociation from the Real. Slipping always between the subject and ideology, between the space of the Real and narrative play, between the Symptom and the Thing, Vollmann's work acts as a sort of contemporary performance piece which emphasizes the slippage rather than the thing itself. It is, finally, self-reflexively concerned with this movement rather than with representation. The temporal moment of acknowledgment—for author and reader—is more significant than its fixed medium of narrative representation.

The performative aspect of Vollmann's work is the reading lesson he provides for the historian of the "discovery" narrative. We cannot renegotiate and find some "true" history. Our own "incorrigible" desire to reincorporate the Real into the reconstruction of narrative must undo our project and, ultimately, always already, risk cultural appropriation—in spite of motives. As postmodern readers in search of the Real, we learn, like Vollmann/SubZero/John Franklin, that it will be our own face that must confront us from beneath the ice as "absolute north," and that the Real will always glimmer elusively just outside our colonial grasp.

Notes

1. See Louise Pratt's *Imperial Eyes: Travel Writing and Transculturation* (London: Routledge, 1992). Pratt's discussion combines ideology and genre critique in a compelling way, though does not confront the subject of the Subject, as do postcolonial critics Homi Bhabha and Abdul JanMohamed.

2. In Larry McCaffery's *In Another Frequency* (Philadelphia: University of Pennsylvania Press, forthcoming), Vollmann explains that his project will ultimately include seven volumes—each corresponding to a particular "dream." Each "dream"

will involve a particular historical moment of European and American intervention in the lives of indigenous peoples. His next volume purportedly concerns Pocahantas and John Smith.

3. Vollmann's "real-life" encounters mark all of the Dream novels, and truly distinguish his work as a hybrid form of fiction, combining enthographic research, personalized or "confessional" narrative, and extensive "on-site" research.

4. In *Lacan* (Cambridge: Harvard University Press, 1991), Malcolm Bowie aptly describes the Lacanian Real as paradoxical—the "unthinkable being thought," which comes close to Jean-François Lyotard's description in *The Postmodern Condition: A Report on Knowledge* (Minneapolis: University of Minneapolis Press, 1979), a definition of the postmodern as the representation of the "unrepresentable."

5. See Michel Foucault's *Discipline and Punish: The Birth of the Prison* (New York: Penguin, 1977).

6. Bowie writes eloquently of the entire legislative processes involved in Lacan's triadic system: "'The signifier' is of course a convenient catch phrase. Lacan uses it, in his papers of the 1950s, as a way of suggesting the existence, within the noise of human language, of a fundamental level of structuration, by recourse to which the manifold flowering of social and cultural forms may be understood. 'The Symbolic' is an equally convenient way of sketching the entire range of those levels, from lowest to highest, and the common structural principles that allow them to intercommunicate" (85). Moreover, as a component of this overdetermining legislative structure, Lacan's "The-Name-of-the-Father" becomes a crucial aspect of the law. "The Name-of-the-Father was a symbol of an authority at once legislative and punitive. It represented, within the Symbolic, that which made the Symbolic possible—all those agencies that placed enduring restrictions on the infant's desire and threatened to punish, by castration, infringements on their law. It was the inaugurating agent of the law, but also gave birth to the mobility and the supple interconnectedness of the signifying chain. Once this fundamental signifier was expelled, the entire process of signification was thrown into disarray" (108).

7. Žižek is especially concerned with the science-fiction genre and the narrative of the extraterrestrial. However, this genre is closely related to the discovery narrative as it seeks to explore the alien Other. Science fiction is in a sense the postmodern form of the discovery narrative.

8. See Fredric Jameson's "Marxism and Historicism" and "Of Islands and Trenches," in *The Ideologies of Theory: Essays, 1971–1986, Syntax of History* (Minneapolis: University of Minnesota Press, 1980). Jameson's notion of the Real finds further articulation in "Imaginary and Symbolic in Lacan," in *The Ideologies of Theory: Volume 1, The Situation of Theory*, as well as more brief references in *The Political Unconscious*. For Jameson, the control of the Real in the context of utopian paradigms is a particular concern.

Works Cited

Cohen, Tom. "Beyond 'The Gaze': Zizek, Hitchcock and the American Sublime." *American Literary History 2*, Vol. 7 (1995): 350–59.

Hutcheon, Linda. *A Theory of Parody: The Teachings of Twentieth-Century Art Forms.* London: Methuen, 1985.

Jameson, Fredric. *The Ideologies of Theory Essays 1971–1986 Volume 2: The Syntax of History*. Minneapolis: University of Minnesota Press, 1988.

———. "Postmodernism: or the Cultural Logic of Late Capitalism." *New Left Review* 146 (July-August 1984): 59–92.

JanMohamed, Abdul R. "The Economy of Manichean Allegory: The Function of Racial Difference in Colonialist Literature." *Critical Inquiry* 12 (1985): 59–88.

Lacan, Jacques. *Ecrits: A Selection*. 1966. Trans. Alan Sheridan. New York: Norton, 1977.

———. The *Four Fundamental Concepts of Psycho-Analysis*. 1973. Trans. Alan Sheridan. New York: Norton, 1978.

Michasiw, Kim. "Camp, Masculinity, Masquerade." *Differences* 6 (1994): 146–73.

Palumbo-Liu, David. "The Minority Self as Other: Problematics of Representation in Asian-American Literature." *Cultural Critique* 28 (1994): 75–102.

Pratt, Mary Louise. *Imperial Eyes: Travel Writing and Transculturation*. New York: Routledge, 1992.

Tyler, Carole-Anne. "Passing: Narcissism, Identity, and Difference." *Differences* 6 (1994): 212–48.

Vollmann, William T. *The Ice Shirts*. New York: Penguin, 1990.

———. *Fathers and Crows*. New York: Viking, 1992.

———. *The Rifles*. New York: Pennguin, 1995.

Žižek, Slavoj. *The Sublime Object of Ideology*. New York: Verso, 1989.

———. *Looking Awry: An Introduction to Jacques Lacan Through Popular Culture*. Cambridge: MIT Press, 1991.

———. *For They Know Not What They Do—Enjoyment as a Political Factor*. New York: Verso, 1991.

CHAPTER THREE

Dancing with the Dead: Ghost Dancing, and Leslie Marmon Silko's *Almanac of the Dead*

They are all dead.   —Leslie Marmon Silko, *Almanac of the Dead*

I am getting ready to speak at length about ghosts, inheritance, generations of ghosts, which is to say about certain others who are not present,
not presently living, either to us or in us or outside us, it is in the name of
justice. Of justice where it is not yet, not yet there. . . . It is necessary to
speak of the ghost, indeed to the ghost and with it. . . . To be just: beyond
the living present in general. . . . A spectral moment, a moment that no
longer belongs to time. . . . This justice carries life beyond present life or
its actual being-there, its empirical or ontological actuality. . . . There is
then some spirit. Spirits. And one must reckon with them. One cannot
not have to . . . and the thing is even more difficult for a reader, a professor, an interpreter, in short . . . a "scholar". . . a traditional scholar doesn't
believe in ghosts—nor in all that which could be called the virtual space
of spectrality.

—Jacques Derrida, *Specters of Marx*

Haunting of History

PLAYED OUT IN the dusty geographies of the western hemispheres—*el
Norte* and south—Silko's complex *Almanac of the Dead* is a fantasy chroni-
cling the demise of the postmodern "Americas."[1] Everywhere in Silko's fictional landscape, things seem to be falling apart. In Arizona, civic order is
collapsing from the drug trade. The elite and the robber barons in Mexico
erect mansions as the homeless die in the streets. A New Mexico film company profanes the sacred while on location in a Laguna Pueblo holy place.
The persistent specter of a mass murderer haunts a wealthy San Diego sub-
urban neighborhood. In Philadelphia, Detroit, Washington, and New

York City, federal troops assemble as state bankruptcy and corruption cause riots to begin among angry citizens.

Though seemingly random, in *Almanac*, these events soon take on the force of a kind of negative manifest destiny. For Silko's Lecha, the mestiza obsessed with the transcription of the cryptic Almanac of the Dead (the fragmentary "history" of indigenous peoples bequeathed to her by her *Yaqui* grandmother), the events have been presaged by the Almanac, which speaks to her softly in "mouths and tongues" (12) about a "world that is about to end" (135). Lecha comes to understand that the approaching apocalypse was the result of what the "white invaders" had done to others. As she puts it: the "tables had turned; now the colonizers were being colonized" (739).

For Lecha, as for the myriad other subversives and misfits inhabiting Silko's mercurial fantasy, the voices and events haunting contemporary America bespeak an alternate reality that resides beyond the traditional categories of Western thought and its manifestation in the colonization of America. *Almanac* ultimately reveals that the ensuing collapse of the "Europeanized" Americas coincides with the fulfillment of the ghost dance prophesy. First envisioned and danced by the Paiute visionary Wovoka in the 1870s, ghost dancing and its apocalyptic vision spread throughout the plains Indians toward the end of the Indian wars. In 1890, more than two hundred Lakota were massacred at Wounded Knee while ghost dancing.[2] Bringing together the ecstatic Indian body, visitations from the dead, visions of the afterlife, and a prayer for survival, the prophesy foresaw a day when the whiteman would vanish and vanquished Indians and their sacred buffalo would return to the once bountiful plains. In the climactic scenes of Silko's novel, Lecha's old warrior friend Wilson Weasel Tale thus invokes the image of Wovoka. He suggests to the gathered subversives that ghost dancing still holds the promise of Indian renewal. There are other voices, he tells his followers, voices that belong to the realm of "dreams and spirits," of "the beloved ancestors lost in the five-hundred-year war" (722). He implores his fellow revolutionaries to return to "the old ways," to dance:

We dance to remember,
we dance to remember all our beloved ones,
to remember how each passed to the spirit world.
We dance because the dead love us,

Weasel Tale ends by talking to the dead, exclaiming: "You are more powerful than memory!" (722).

In "Native American Indian Literature: Critical Metaphors of the Ghost Dance," Gerald Vizenor addresses how ghost dancing might provide a profound metaphor for contemporary Native American writers of imaginative literature. He contends that, while English and American narratives of the West construct the traditional language of colonization, the narrative of the ghost dance provides an alternative vocabulary through which this colonial process might be subverted. Writes Vizenor:

English has been the language of colonial discoveries, racial cruelties, invented names, and the written domination of tribal cultures; at the same time this mother tongue of neocolonialism has been a language of liberation for some people. English, learned under duress by tribal people at mission and federal schools, was one of the languages that carried the ghost dance . . . English, the coercive language at federal boarding schools, has carried some of the best stories of endurance and tribal spiritual restoration . . . The characters dance as tricksters, a stature that would unite tribal memories. The language of tribal novelists and poets could be a literary ghost dance, a literature of liberation that enlivens tribal survival. (277)

As a "literary ghost dance," *Almanac* apprehends this process of reclamation in its fantastic projection of an apocalyptic end of "white history."

In terms resonant with Vizenor's suggestion that ghost dancing provides an alternate expression of tribal memories, Jacques Derrida, in his *Specters of Marx*, explores the notion of ghosts and the disruption of history and comes finally to a theory of "hauntology," a way of representing the unrepresentable in history.[3] There can be no justice, no simile of truth or good faith, argues Derrida, without seeking a voice or space for the absent. And because the absent—by their very nature—are not present, they are denied hegemonic representation. The result is that history is haunted: the ineffable, the unrepresentable, the unknowable howl at the borders of consciousness and undermine narrative. "Hegemony still organizes the repression, and thus the confirmation of a haunting," argues Derrida, and thus, "haunting belongs to the structure of every hegemony" (37). History, the very record of this hegemony, is problematized and deconstructed by these specters.

What, then, does it mean to write a history of the West, particularly amid the "media parade of current discourse on the end of history" (Derrida 15)? How does one arrange the images of the dead to allow voice for the absent? How does one write a history at the end of history? How can the unrepresentable process of hauntology, which must visit any just history, be expressed?

While these troublesome questions afflict much of postmodernism and are central to any discussion of western literature, they are the focus of

Silko's counter-history. As a postmodern "literary Ghost Dance," Silko's *Almanac of the Dead* indeed proves "haunting," in Derrida's sense, presenting us with an alternative story of "tribal memory" and survival. Moreover, its complicated literary landscape, influenced by the tropes of ghost dancing—Indian bodies, communing with the dead, violent confrontations with the Other, counter-memory—suggests the important ways in which ghost dancing serves as both a sacred ritual and a political act of resistance and survivance in postmodern Native American "literature of liberation." But before turning to Silko's text and considering precisely how it "turns the tables" on colonial representations, it is necessary to return for a moment to the historical coding of ghost dancing at Wounded Knee and its figuration in two famous texts. Ethnographer James Mooney's *The Ghost Dance Religion and Sioux Outbreak of 1890* and Lakota holy man Black Elk's historical and sacred teachings illustrate the centrality of the dance to ensuing history and explain the return of the dance within the context of 1970s political activism.

Silenced Bodies and the Historic Ghost Dancers

A famous photograph indelibly marks the violent collision between the U.S. military and the Lakota at Wounded Knee. Black and white, hauntingly violent, silent, an official document of the Smithsonian Institute—the terrifying photograph represents the vanquished ghost dancers of Wounded Knee. Taken on the ice-scaped fields of Dakota, the photograph is meant to officially document the death of over two hundred dancers killed on December 17, 1890, by the triumphant Seventh Cavalry. The stasis of the photo—the unmoving frozen bodies, stacked on the windblown field—makes it seem as though the bodies are part of some unreachable past, an ethnographical scene displaced from its context, emptied of its content.[4]

The photograph is an "official" document associated with the official narrative of ethnographer James Mooney, a representative of the bureau of ethnography. Mooney's *The Ghost Dance Religion and the Sioux Outbreak of 1890* is widely considered to be a kind of ethnographic master narrative of the massacre. As an inaugural report, Mooney's text offers a glimpse at the colonial forces brought to bear on the Lakota. As an "interpretation" of not only the Lakota ghost dance religion and the ghost dancing itself, Mooney's account also stands in marked contrast to another famous "interpretation" of the massacre, that offered by the Lakota holy man Black Elk.[5]

The two most widely read articulations of Black Elk's narrative are John Neihart's *Black Elk Speaks* (subsequently followed by his *When the Tree Flowered*) and the more recent work by Raymond DeMallie, *The Sixth Grandfather*. While both works are seminal and similar, DeMallie's edition provides a larger, more complete context for Black Elk's narrative, and in consequence, is the text referenced here. As artifacts, these two accounts—the "official" narrative of the ghost dance religion and Black Elk's oral history—point to the ways that the Lakota's perception of the ghost dance, the Wounded Knee massacre, history, and the world itself diverged from mainstream Anglo-American conceptions.

As an ethnologist working under John Wesley Powell, then chief of the newly formed bureau of ethnography, Mooney was sent to Dakota to study the ghost dance, and to calculate its part in the massacre.[6] Powell was determined to Christianize the Indians so that they might eventually find their places within the "new phase of Aryan civilization" being developed in America. An avid assimilationist, Powell articulated a belief that "primitive Indians" could be aculturated and assimilated into Anglo culture through "social evolution" (Mooney 27). Though Mooney himself was sympathetic to the cultural differences that made the recalcitrant Lakota, in his words, an "anathema to the American people," he nonetheless carried with him a view not dissimilar to that held by Powell, a view vis-à-vis the Indian and the larger project of Christianization.

In his account, Mooney traces the "origins" of the dance to its first enactment by the Nevada Paiute Wovoka in the 1870s, from where it spread to numerous other tribes, and then ultimately to the embattled Lakota. In describing the actual dance, Mooney attempts to be resolutely objective. He records carefully the colorful clothing, the position of the sun, and the "frenzied" movements of the tribes within the sacred circle. But in narrativizing the "meaning" of the dance and its attendant prophecy, Mooney's account clearly reflects the valence of the author's humanistic Christian/colonial perspective.

As Derrida's theory of "hauntology" in *Specters of Marx* asserts, the repressed must always return and haunt homogeneous discourse. The "scholar," Derrida argues, is particularly unsuited and unable to identify the haunting specter, for scholars are of necessity trained in a finite, disciplinary vocabulary. Scholars do not converse with specters, and Mooney, for all his good intentions, cannot speak with ghosts. His empirical tools do not embrace either spectral actuality or the alternate spirituality and historicism of Native Americans.

As he explains in a section aptly entitled "The Narrative: Paradise Lost," Mooney ultimately interprets the ghost dance movement as reflexive with the "great" religious movements. "The doctrines of the Hindu avatar," writes Mooney, along with "the Hebrew Messiah, the Christian millennium, and the Hesunanin of the Indian Ghost dance are essentially the same, and have their origin in a home and longing common to all humanity" (657). Reading the ghost dance as a Christian allegory, Mooney suggests that it concerns the quest that "probably every Indian tribe, north and south had . . ." the quest to find "a person of dignified presence, a father and teacher of his children, a very Christ . . . who gathers the wandering nomads" (658). Thus, one of the most significant spiritual movements of nineteenth-century Native Americans was translated into Anglican Christian discourse.

Interviewing participating Indians from his own religious perspective, Mooney was rapidly convinced that the "true" nature of the new messiah was being revealed to him. "As I had always shown a sympathy for their ideas and feelings," writes Mooney, "and now accomplished a long journey to the messiah himself at the cost of considerable difficulty and hardship, the Indians were at last fully satisfied that I was really desirous of learning the truth of their new religion" (780). Mooney's search for "truth," however, ultimately leads him to conclude that the ghost dance movement represents not so much a "new religion" as an evolutionary step in "bringing the savage into civilization" (783). Correspondingly, he concludes by viewing the movement—and dance—not so much as an accepted site of cultural difference, but as a transitional episode in the forward progress of Indian Christianization and assimilation:

In conclusion, we may say of the prophet and his doctrine what has been said of one of his apostles by a careful and competent investigator: "He has given these people a better religion than they ever had before, taught them precepts which, if faithfully carried out, will bring them into better accord with their white neighbors, and has prepared the way for their final Christianization. (783)

Wovoka was reinscribed as an apostle, and the ghost dance—the prayer that waited for the removal of whites from the continent—became to a large extent for Mooney a gesture of accommodation.

In contrast to Mooney's *Ghost Dance Religion*, Black Elk's oral narrative of events suggests a very different history associated with the silencing of the Indian body. By 1889, Black Elk recalled, the Lakota nation was deeply troubled and impoverished. The much contested Black Hills treaty had been broken, and the promises of the "Waichus" (whites) had proven empty. In the wake of treachery and starvation, rumors reached the tribe of Jack Wilson, called Wovoka. A prophet who lived in Mason Valley, Nevada, Wovoka informed his visitors: "They should . . . have a Ghost Dance, and in doing this they would save themselves, that there is another world coming—a world just for the Indians, that in time the world would come and crush out all the whites" (DeMallie 257). Slowly this instruction, with its appeal for the resurrection of the "old ways," made its way to Pine Ridge and Cheyenne Creek.

In part because of the widespread despair and poverty, the Lakota people were open to some alternative spiritual vision. Black Elk reports that "there was quite a famine among the people and some of them really believed this Messiah business and were hoping that this land of promise would come soon" (DeMallie 264). Three men, says Black Elk—God Thunder, Brave Bear, and Yellow Breast—traveled west in search of this "Messiah." The men returned with instructions regarding the performance of the ghost dance and brought back sacred items. A few months later, another group of men went in search of Wovoka. When they returned, Kicking Bear held the first Lakota ghost dance at Cheyenne Creek, just north of Pine Ridge. Recalls Black Elk: "Something seemed to tell me to go and I resisted it for a while but then I could no longer resist, so I got on my horse and went to this Ghost Dance," (DeMallie 258). For Black Elk, the performance of the ghost dance led to revelation.

One of the most striking elements of Black Elk's narrative is his insistence that the gestures and visionary experiences associated with the ghost dance were prefigured in his childhood dreams. When Black Elk was nine, he had fallen seriously ill and, while seemingly inert and unconscious, experienced a series of visions. In these dreams, Black Elk spoke with his ancestors—the six grandfathers—and left his corporeal body so that he might glimpse the universe in much larger and utopian manner. At the center of Black Elk's vision was a flowering stick and "the sacred hoop" that represented the interconnectedness of the world (DeMallie 111–28). Although unable to express this vision upon waking, the young Black Elk was marked and changed by the power of his dream. Strangely, as he experienced the ghost dance, this past vision reasserted itself.

The words that Black Elk uses to describe the ghost dance are clear and detailed, remarking on both the return of his vision and upon the primacy of bodies in the dance. Notes Black Elk as he watches the dancers:

They had a sacred pole in the center. It was a circle in which they were dancing and I could clearly see that this was my sacred hoop and in the center they had an exact duplicate of my tree that never blooms . . . it came to my mind that perhaps with this power the tree would bloom and the people would get the sacred hoop again. It seemed that I could recall all of my vision in it. . . . It was all from my vision. (DeMallie 258)

This sense of recollection was to stay with Black Elk, supporting his feeling that he was meant to be an "intercessor on earth" for his people.

A day after first watching the dance, Black Elk anointed himself with red paint and joined the dancing bodies that moved about the sacred pole. He describes a dance of bodies clasping hands, raising and lowering their connected arms, moving constantly in a circle. As the participants became increasingly absorbed in the dance, they would alternately laugh, weep, gasp, and scream. Struck by the "power," various dancers would release the hands they held, stagger, shout, and finally fall to the ground:

As we started to dance again, some of the people would be laughing And some would be crying. Some of them would lie down for a vision and we just kept on dancing. I could see more of them staggering around panting and then they would fall down for visions. The people were crying for the old ways of living and that their religion would be with them again. (DeMallie 260)

The account of the ecstatic, often otherworldly vision of the ghost dance is marked with the bodily movements of its participants.

The physical terms that Black Elk uses to describe the dance are striking. His recollections are filled with recorded sensation. The Indian body—as the agent of an expansive representation of reality—is crucial to Black Elk's narrative. Unlike Mooney, who relied upon scholarly training and the narrative structures of Christianity in order to explain the dance, Black Elk understands the "truth" of the dance through the medium of his own body. He writes about his body with a language that is far removed from Mooney's. "At the first dance I had no vision but my body seemed to be raised off the ground while I danced and I had a queer feeling," says Black Elk (DeMallie 260). Later he remembers:

It took quite a while for me to get in this condition. They sang all sorts of songs. Then I began to fear that my breath was coming up while we were dancing. The first feeling that I had was that my legs seemed to be full of ants. . . . It seemed as though I were swaying off the ground without touching it. This queer feeling came up farther and it was in my heart now . . . it seemed that I would glide forward like a swing and swing back again. . . . My arms were outstretched and right before me I could see a spotted eagle dancing toward me. . . . I glided over. (DeMallie 261)

This is the vision that Black Elk also remembers from his initial dreams when he was nine. The repetition of the image struck Black Elk and his people as significant and holy. Eventually, Black Elk became a spiritual leader of his tribe and those who participated in the ghost dance.

"Let us live," Black Elk beseeched the great spirit. The vision of the dance seemed to offer another historic possibility for the Lakota. Perhaps the dancing bodies reflected a desire for a better future. The Indian bodies bent and writhed in search of some other narrative besides the familiar story of western expansion and the eradication of the native. Wrapped in their protective, painted ghost shirts—shirts that originated in another of Black Elk's dreams—the Indians danced their counter-history. But, quickly, the dance was made illegal and the subversive dancing bodies were silenced. The dancing Indian bodies moving in waves had longed for a more hopeful history, but another history was recorded. American history required the breaking and erasure of the Indian body. History, counter-history, and the ghost dance would be reduced to photographs, displays at wild west shows, and material for avid anthropologists.

Significantly, nearly a hundred years after it emerged, ghost dancing re-emerged as a form of resistance in the 1970s, further inscribing the dance with a revolutionary aura. Numerous Lakota activists—Russell Means, Leonard Peltier, and Mary Crow Dog, among them—began ghost dancing as a way of rekindling "the old ways" and establishing "Indian unity" (*Lakota* 153).[7] Because ghost dancing at this historical juncture resulted in armed conflict between Indians and agents of the goverment, it marked a recoding of ghost dancing within the context of resistance and political activism. Dancing at Wounded Knee, activists engaged in "the language of liberation" (to use Vizenor's phrase) and resisted colonization and laws that prohibited Indian bodies from dancing the ghost dance.

But for Black Elk, and for his fellow Native Americans, the vision of communal possibility was erased by the advance of Anglo-American militarism and the march of white history. Their voices are silenced within the hegemonic record of American history. The ghost dancers retreated, and, with them, their bodily record of tribal history evaporated. The history of the Other was silenced, but it is this history that Silko's text summons.

Literary Ghost Dance

Almanac of the Dead has vast resonances with both the historic occasion of the ghost dance and the body politic of contemporary ghost dancers. The literal evocation of the ghost dance is pivotal to the text, as is the unifying prophesy of the dance: the vision that the Indian nations will once again arise and the Anglo race disappear from the continent. But perhaps more significantly, *Almanac* explores those complex and subtle issues that have structured the minority experience of the west, and that, of course, find representation in the dance. The nontraditional interpretation of death, the fragmentation of history, and the image of the trickster playing perpetually at the borders of consciousness are all operative themes within Silko's text. Like the dance, the novel eschews the often bifurcated quality of Anglo-American consciousness. It is a story about another way to read the narrative of the American west, and the lexicon of this alternative representation lies in the ghost dancing itself.

Silko's *Almanac* possesses a labyrinthine structure, one that defies conventional analysis. The book is nearly impossible to summarize; it is too long, too convoluted, and too much mired in the presentation of alternate viewpoints. But while some readers may condemn this narrative as confused, this confusion is, in fact, precisely the point Silko's text seeks to make. The hierarchies of conventional narrative structures have been dissolved. Because Silko's account is a kind of counter-narrative, it is free to ignore such conventions as linear development of plot, clarity of thesis, and narrative unity. This narrative complexity is emblematic of both Silko's text and the Native American culture that she explores. It is multifaceted and multivoiced, resistant to facile assumptions and literary focus.

Almanac of the Dead is no ordinary almanac. It is a catalogue that finally notes the absurdity of cataloging. Silko eschews the presence of a single narrator or a single narrative point of view. The novel weaves together varying ways of seeing, varying histories, and varied forms of consciousness. The reader is left with an anarchistic aesthetic—that is to say, all principles of unity are disarranged. The novel is ultimately a kind of collage, a work that undermines narrative convention. This literary revolution is based on more than sensibility. As Silko revives history and awakens the dead, any progressive notion of time is destroyed, and, as classical rhetoric instructs, without clear notions regarding temporality, linear narrative is liberated. As the single controlling narrative position is fragmented—interrupted by a host of other voices and perspectives—narrative authority is subverted.

Like Silko's *Almanac*, ghost dancing operated within an alternate aesthetic, an aesthetic that undermined any vision of centralized authorial perspective. Just as Silko's characters and historic visions each have their own story, so the ghost dance's participants each claimed their own performative space. In both texts, the principle of aesthetic unity is destroyed. This narrative anarchism resonates with the themes of Silko's novel.

In *Almanac*, Silko's "white" characters, though haunted by the "voices of the dead," seemingly have no access to such a narrative. Rather, like Seese, the "blonde" woman who has lost her child and has enlisted Lecha to find her through her communications with the dead, they can only push at the edges of some awareness of an alternate reality behind the unraveling of things.

For example, after the suicide of her friend Eric, Seese can only suspect that an alternate reading of events exists. Like the dreams and voices that haunt her, her understanding is ephemeral, necessarily limited by her acculturation in European traditions of regarding the dead. English has limits here, and Seese has no vocabulary with which to understand:

Sometimes a voice inside Seese's head cried out . . . to Eric, "Why did you kill yourself. Is that what you do to the people who love you?" But she understood exactly why you might do that to the ones you loved. So then gradually, from the grief and the anger, Seese had come to feel that she was no more alive than Eric was. That in death she and Eric would always be bound together—sister and brother. There did not seem to be a vocabulary for what they had felt. Or if there had been a vocabulary, she hadn't understood it. (58)

In contrast, Silko's mestiza Lecha understands that the dead who speak are spirits awaiting liberation.[8] Like Black Elk, she moves freely between the two worlds that await conversion after the ensuing apocalypse. But as a possessor of *la conciencia de Mestiza*, Lecha is burdened by a double reading of history and reality. Alternately positioned in what Emily Hicks has called two cultural codes, she is obviously aware of the competing narratives of Indians and whites. While she understands that the entropic decline that characterizes the present will evolve into the hoped for salvation of the ghost dance, she nonetheless feels the pain of the whites who do not understand the horrible transpiring of events. Amid the ruination of the "Americas," Lecha sadly acknowledges that "they are all dead. The only ones you can locate are the dead. Murder victims and suicides. You can't locate the living. If you find them they will be dead. Those who have lost loved ones only come to you to confirm their sorrow" (139).

Lecha knows that for the "whites," who do not comprehend the Indian prophesy, the dead will remain as "fragments of bone burnt to ash, or long strands of hair," that "move in the ocean wind as it shifts the sand across the dunes" (139). Only through her focus on Indian prophesy and the "Indian way" does Lecha make sense of the ensuing destruction and come to realize that the approaching apocalypse and cultural failure should not create anxiety. Another history—the great history predicted in the ghost dance—is about to commence:

The message was quite simple. There was nothing to fear or to worry about. People should go about their daily routines. Because already the great shift of human populations on the continents was underway and there was nothing human beings could do to stop it. Conflicts and collisions were inevitable, but it was best to start from scratch anyway. Nothing European in the Americas had worked very well anyway except destruction . . . Converts were always welcome; Mother Earth embraced the souls of all who loved her. No fences or walls, would stop them; guns and bombs would not stop them. They had no fear of death. (736)

Freed from these temporal concerns, and able to sense another discourse and history, Lecha's consciousness can move beyond the meaningless and impoverished modern world. This shift in historic consciousness can only be read by Lecha through her body and spirit; it lies outside western European thought.

Silko's dissolution of the discreet separation between life and death has other ramifications. For without death as an ordering principle, conventional ideas of time and history are similarly dissolved. If there is no barrier between life and death, between the physical and spiritual worlds—and if the dead can freely occupy the world of the living—then narrative progress, as well as progressive conceptions of history, become meaningless constructs. In allying itself with the spirituality of the dance, Silko's text is no longer confined by temporal narrative. Moreover, the rupture between Indian and western conceptions of time is resonant with a broader critique in Silko's text of official narratives of history in the west. This critique becomes clear in Silko's portrayal of the oppositional readings of history by the characters of Laguna Sterling and the revolutionary La Escapia.

Displaced from his New Mexico homeland, Sterling ends up at Zeta and Lecha's Tucson ranch, where he develops an abiding interest in alternate forms of history. Having grown up in government boarding schools, where "history teachers seldom got them past the American Civil War" (40), Sterling instead learns history from old *Reader's Digests* and pulp detective and crime magazines. Favorite among the articles are the "Yesteryear Files" (74), which romantically re-create "history and stuff" (75). From these, Sterling develops a fondness for his two favorite men, John Dillinger and Geronimo, whose romantic portrayals as "tricked" men make them strangely alike. Similarly, Sterling develops numerous theories about the justice system based solely on his reading of the magazines, theories which though they sound bizarre, have credence within the context of the "alternate" history Silko presents in *Almanac*.

In her depiction of Sterling's pulp magazine-constructed past, Silko comically suggests that, like reality, all narrative history is, in Richard Rorty's phrase, "radically contingent." Sterling's history is thus no less valid than the "official" narratives he learned in the government schools. Moreover, Sterling's magazine history does not develop as a monologue, but develops instead through his reading a range of disjunctive and fragmentary "stories" about history. Consequently, the magazines implicitly force Sterling to remain skeptical about any absolute "truth" regarding historical narrative. Ironically, Sterling's magazine-reality leads him to question laws based on such relative notions as "truth" and "justice," and the very idea of what it means to be a "criminal":

Sterling fell asleep wondering if Mexico had produced any criminals as outstanding as John Dillinger or Pretty Boy Floyd. His knowledge of Mexican history was sketchy, but Sterling did not think they had anyone like Geronimo or Montezuma. And then it got very confusing because it seemed as if the Mexicans were always having revolutions, and he knew that although the winning side usually executed and jailed the losers for being "criminals," both *Police Gazette* and *True Detective* magazines disqualified crimes committed during wars and revolutions. (89)

Though more lyrical, the revolutionary La Escapia's revisioning of Marx as a "magic storyteller" similarly amounts to a radically contingent alternate reading of history. Out of her unique experience as a mestiza, La Escapia constructs Marx as resonant with her own cosmology. "Tribal people," she announces, "had all the experience they would ever need to judge whether Marx's stories told the truth" (310). In her notebooks, which like Lecha's consist of fragmentary scribbling, La Escapia thus "writes" Marx as a prescient "Indian" seer, who is virulently anti-European. She notes: "The Indians had seen generations of themselves ground into bloody pulp under the steel wheels of ore cars in crumbling tunnels of gold mines. The Indians had seen for themselves the cruelty of the Europeans towards children and women. That was how La Escapia had satisfied herself Marx was reliable; his accounts had been consistent with what the people already knew" (312). La Escapia's reality coincides with the world Marx described so many years before. Her inchoate, intuitive, and repressed history is the history of revolution.[9]

Moreover, La Escapia believes Marx, like herself, "understood the stories of the people" or their "history had always been sacred" (315). Marx's need to retell the stories of the marginal came from a desire to prevent the people from becoming "lost." "This man Marx," she knows, "had understood that the stories or 'histories' are sacred; that within 'history' reside relentless forces, powerful spirits, vengeful, relentlessly seeking justice" (316). Consequently, La Escapia's mystical imaging of Marx as a visionary, reinvents him, not as a godless theoretician, but rather as a deeply spiritual friend of the Indians who ultimately is betrayed by European values:

La Escapia imagined Marx as a storyteller who worked feverishly to gather together a magical assembly of stories to cure the suffering and evils of the world by the retelling of the stories. . . . Marx . . . and his associates had been wrong about so many other things because they were Europeans to start with, and anything, certainly any philosophy, would have been too feeble to curb the greed and sadism of centuries. (316)

Developed from her unique perspective, La Escapia's view of Marx thus resists "traditional" representations. Rather, it underscores Silko's argument that "history" is a narrative that is radically contingent depending on one's perspective. As Marx recounted in *The German Ideology*, representation within discourse and dominant ideology—history, if you will—is largely a "conjurer's trick," dependent upon a prevailing image or ghost. The silencing of those outside of hegemonic discourse represents a sort of theft, a theft of the subject of the self.

Like Sterling and La Escapia's representations of "reality," as well as those provided by Black Elk, Silko's *Almanac* ultimately calls into question what constitutes history. In its fusion of myth, fiction, alternative and straight "history," Native American spiritualism into what might be considered a postmodern pastiche of history, it implicitly suggests that from within the margins of these generic categories, a different history is possible. *Almanac* raises the issue of agency, its text suggesting that narrative authority is always a question of power. For Silko, the silencing of the Indian voice, reflected in the violence confronting the ghost dancers, is coextensive with discursive traditions that have denied indigenous people agency within colonial historical narratives.

The critique of "truth," which extends into the realm of "history" and ethnographic authority, decenters interpretation and categorical distinctions between truth, fiction, history, and myth. Marginal readings of historical reality, such as Sterling's and La Escapia's thus become equally "valid" interpretations of events. From this perspective, Mooney's ethnographic master narrative is no more valid than that provided by Black Elk. Silko's *Almanac*, in its complex way, thus attempts to free itself from the monologue that has come to embody much of the history of the American frontier. Like the ghost dance, *Almanac* is about the presence of other/"Other" voices. The novel asserts itself against the valence of "traditional history" and what Michel de Certeau has called the "writing that conquers" (227).

Body Talk

In "The Metaphysics of Writing Indian-White History," Calvin Martin stresses that Indian history must be written differently than white history. "If we are to understand the contemporary Indian we must first understand the historic Indian," comments Martin. "That means giving him an historic voice" (153–59). While this is undeniably so, the reinvocation of the ghost dance by AIM (American Indian Movement) members asserts itself as a performance of "history" that in some ways can never coincide with the cerebral narrativity of "white history" through the employment of the body. In this sense, bodily gestures displace history. In *Heterologies: Discourse on the Other*, Michel de Certeau extends Russell Means's comment that "Indians have a long memory," by suggesting: "This history of resistance punctuated by cruel repression is marked on the Indian's body as much as it is recorded in transmitted accounts—or more so. . . . In this sense, the body is memory. . . . A unity born of hardship and resistance to hardship is the historical locus, the collective memory of the social body" (227).[10] Silko's *Almanac* correspondingly gives much play to the trope of the body, and the embodiment of Indian history. The voices that haunt the text, that speak in "whispers and tongues," seemingly remain detached from the corporeal world. They are specters, awaiting connection—history awaiting embodiment.

Crucial to Silko's imaging of the body as a central site of "social memory" is her depiction of Lecha's relation to the ancient almanac passed to her by her grandmother Yeome. As Yeome tells her, "I have kept the notebooks and the old book since it was passed on to me many years ago. A section of one of the notebooks had accidentally been lost right before they were given to me" (128). In giving Lecha the task of "translating" and restoring the old text, Yeome stresses that "the problem has been the meaning of the lost section and for me to find a way of replacing it. . . . The woman warned that it should not be just any sort of words" (128). Then Yeome confides:

I am telling you this because you must understand how carefully the old manuscripts and its notebooks must be kept. Nothing must be added that was not already there. Only repairs are allowed, and one might live as long as I have and not find a suitable code. (128)

Indeed, Lecha is left to consider for the remainder of the novel the "problem" of the ancient almanac.

But hidden within Yeome's story of her tribe's desperate struggle to pre-serve the history of her people, are Silko's carefully given clues to the secret of the code. As Yeome details, when the "white invaders" all but wiped out the tribe, the elders sent the almanac north with a group of children. On their arduous quest the children were forced to ingest fragments of the narrative, which they reluctantly cooked into a stew. Yeome points out that in the broth, the "thin brittle page gradually began to change. Brownish ink rose in clouds. Outlines of the letters smeared and they floated up and away like flocks of small birds. . . . Well, it was a wonderful stew. They lived on it for days" (248).

The past is not only consuming, it is consumed. As Yeome's story im-plies, the key to the lost fragments of the past lies necessarily in the body, a wordless entity that must become the literal repository of tribal history. Thus, when Lecha sees Weasel Tale invoke the ghost dance, she implicitly understands that the dancing Indian body is fundamental to Indian regen-eration and the preservation/haunting of ancient secrets.

Near the conclusion of *Almanac* Weasel Tale calls for reclaiming of the ghost dance and chastizes his followers: "You cry the white man has stolen everything, killed all your animals and food. But where were you when people first discussed the Europeans. Tell the truth. You forgot everything you were ever told" (721). He goes on to discuss with the assembled crowd whether or not "the spirits of the ancestors in some way failed our people when the prophets called them to the Ghost Dance" (723). Weasel Tale's explanation is clear: contemporary Native Americans and would-be "In-dians" had been too indoctrinated by European narratives of rationality. They had become "poisoned." Explaining the pervasive mindset of the Eu-ropeans that gradually influenced Native Americans, Weasel Tale sites Mooney's narrative of the ghost dance as emblematic. Weasel Tale expli-citly notes the misreading of Native American history proposed by Moo-ney and his fellow anthropologists and historians, and argues:

Anthropologists alleged the Ghost Dance disappeared because the people became disillusioned when the ghost shirts did not stop bullets and the Europeans did not vanish overnight. But it was the Europeans, not the Native Americans, who had ex-pected results overnight; the anthropologists, who feverishly sought magic objects to postpone their own deaths, had misunderstood the power of the ghost shirts. . . .The ghost shirts have the dancers spiritual protection while the white man dreamed of shirts that repelled bullets because they feared death. (723)

Because Native Americans understood death as simply another kind of history, and could interact with ghosts, unlike Mooney who understood death in entirely Western terms, the ghost dance and its ghost shirts had an entirely different message of a different kind of salvation. Thus Weasel Tale insists to his followers that ghost dancing lies outside the domain of European inscriptions. It cannot be understood by Anglo-European culture, but it is the record of Indian spirituality. Indians must "dance to remember" (723).

Ultimately, Silko's prominent positioning of ghost dancing within her text—a text that argues that contemporary Native Americans must resist the Eurocentric colonial narratives, which seek to erase the Indian voice—suggests that the Indian body has the power to write itself, to speak the unspeakable of history—"to remember." For Silko, ghost dancing provides a postmodern metaphor that resides and performs beyond the scope of the anthropologist's spyglass, and the historian's journal. Indeed, in *Almanac of the Dead*, it provides a way of representing the unrepresentable as it engages in a "literature of liberation that enlivens tribal survival" ("Critical" 227).

Notes

1. These ideas were first presented at a three-month colloquium convened at University of California Riverside's Center for Ideas and Society in 1994 The colloquium was headed by Gayatri Chakavorty Spivak, and I am grateful to her for her valuable commentary. I would also like to thank Susan Foster, professor of dance at the University of California at Riverside.

2. This figure is widely disputed—many Native American scholars put the figure closer to three hundred or four hundred.

3. While many Native American scholars dismiss Derrida—indeed, poststructuralism in general—as overly Eurocentric, I believe this is based on a misreading of Derrida's contribution in terms of multiculturalism. Derrida's celebrated attack on "truth-effects" and "gran-récits," which emerged in the '70's, indeed has opened the way for legitimation of alternative voices and narratives within the realm of theory and critical discourse. "Hauntology" then, can be read as part of Derrida's continuing attack on hegemonic structures, which elide and silence in the process of establishing epistemological and ontological claims.

4. Richard Drinnon, *in Facing West: The Metaphysics of Indian Hating and Empire Building* (New York: Schocken Books, 1990) argues that the cultural impact of this photo was great. He suggests that the image of the silenced ghost dancers on the windblown field had the impact of the photos of the My Lai massacre in later times.

5. John Neihart interviewed Black Elk over a period of years Many of the notes and interviews were transcribed by Neihart's daughters. Moved by Black Elk's account, Neihart became a kind of adopted son to Black Elk and spent many years of his life recounting Black Elk's words and visions. However, historians suggest that Neihart edited and shaped Black Elk's remembrances to conform with literary—and some might say historical and spiritual—stylistic conventions. Certainly it is true that Neihart edited and reduced his lengthy conversational material. Further, Neihart moved certain sections and moments of Black Elk's recollections in order

to create a more smooth, linear, and some might say Anglo, history. Some critics have regarded Neihart's editing and intervention in the text as a well-meant appropriation, while others have questioned the "authenticity" of Neihart's resulting texts. Raymond DeMallie's examination of Black Elk's narrative notes the editorial problems and confronts the issue of "authenticity." DeMallie's text includes complete interviews, notes, and a critical introduction that addresses the problems inherent in oral history, transcription, and interpretation.

6. Mooney himself was an amazing figure, in most ways sympathetic to Indian causes. An early practitioner of "going Native," he often participated with Indians in sacred rituals, and many tribes had great respect for him.

7. The confrontation between Native Americans—in particular, members of the Lakota tribe—and the U.S. government have been well documented in numerous reports. In her troubling remembrance, Mary Crow Dog in *Lakota Woman* (New York: Harper Perennial, 1990) details her own awakening within the context of Wounded Knee and activism on the Pine Ridge reservation in the 1970s. Pine Ridge became a flash point for conflict between AIM activists and the FBI, in the wake of the corrupt reservation governance of Dick Wilson. In *Agents of Repression* (Boston: South End Press, 1988), Ward Churchill and Jim Wall argue that in the '70s Pine Ridge unrest—and by extension ghost dancing—came to symbolize for authorities a central site of Native American resistance: "By the 1970's, the incipient conflict was coming to a head. Not unnaturally, in an era marked by irregular warfare and covert operations both at home and abroad, the government began to weigh its options in terms of possible clandestine alternatives. . . . Regardless of other factors, it was perceived in some sectors of the federal bureaucracy that the time had come to resolve once and for all the issue of the recalcitrant Lakota, a people who had, after all, administered deep and lasting wounds to U.S. martial pride. Here, the logical target would be the Oglalas of Pine Ridge, the segment of the Great Sioux Nation that had all along been viewed—perhaps correctly—as the keystone of Lakota nationalism and resistance" (118). Eventually this tension erupted in the infamous shootout on June, 26, 1975, which resulted in the death of two FBI officers and the subsequent imprisonment of Leonard Peltier. After a celebrated trial, in which William Kunstler defended Peltier, Peltier was found guilty, though a grand jury later determined that there had been falsification of evidence by the government against Peltier. Since then, much controversy has occurred over the actual identity of the assailant, a Lakota man who has reputedly admitted his part in the shooting. See also Peter Matthiessen's *In the Spirit of Crazy Horse* (New York: Viking Press, 1991). These events have also inspired the documentary film *Incident at Oglala*, directed by Michael Apted.

8. In *Borderlands/La Frontera* (San Francisco: Aunt Lute Books, 1987), Gloria Andalzua defines la mestiza as a transcultural border-crosser. "The new mestiza," writes Andalzua, "copes by developing a tolerance for contradictions, a tolerance for ambiguity. She learns to be an Indian in Mexican culture, to be Mexican from an Anglo point of view. She learns to juggle cultures. She has plural personality, she operates in a pluralistic mode—nothing is thrust out, the good, the bad, the ugly, nothing rejected, nothing abandoned. Not only does she sustain contradictions, she turns the ambivalence into something else" (79).

9. Derrida's argument in *Specters of Marx: The State of the Debt, the Work of Mourning, and the New International* (London: Routledge, 1994) comes quite close to Silko's in *Almanac*. Marx is framed in both as an ethical philosopher concerned with justice—and his philosophy of capital simply reflects an expression of his desire to

"do right by the Other," which is how Gayatri Chakavorty Spivak defines the ethical context.

10. See Elaine Scarry's *The Body in Pain* (New York: Oxford University Press, 1985) for discussion of the ideology of pain, which has many resonances with Means's comments.

Works Cited

Churchhill, Ward, and Jim Uanda Wall. *Agents of Repression.* Boston: South End Press, 1988.

Clifford, James. *The Predicament of Culture.* Cambridge: Harvard University Press, 1988.

Crow Dog, Mary. *Lakota Woman.* New York: Harper Perennial, 1990.

de Certeau, Michel. *Heterologies: Discourse on the Other.* Minneapolis: University of Minnesota Press, 1986.

DeMallie, Raymond J. "The Lakota Ghost Dance: An Ethnohistorical Account." *Pacific Historical Review* 4, November 1982.

———. *The Sixth Grandfather: Black Elk's Teachings as Given to John G. Neihart.* Lincoln: University of Nebraska Press, 1984.

Derrida, Jacques. *Specters of Marx: The State of the Debt, the Work of Mourning, and the New International.* London: Routledge Press, 1994.

Drinnon, Richard. *Facing West: The Metaphysics of Indian Hating and Empire Building.* New York: Schocken Books, 1990.

Martin, Calvin. "The Metaphysics of Writing Indian/White History." *Ethnography,* Vol. 26, No. 2, spring 1979.

Matthiessen, Peter. *In the Spirit of Crazy Horse.* New York: Viking Press, 1991.

Mooney, James. *The Ghost Dance Religion and the Sioux Outbreak of 1890.* Albuquerque: Rio Grande Press, 1973.

Neidhadt, John G. *Black Elk Speaks: Being the Life Story of a Holy Man of the Oglala Sioux as Told Through John G. Neihardt.* Lincoln: University of Nebraska Press, 1979.

Silko, Leslie Marmon. *Almanac of the Dead.* New York: Simon and Schuster, 1991.

Vizenor, Gerald. *Narrative Chance: Postmodern Discourse and Native American Indian Literatures.* Albuquerque: University of New Mexico Press, 1989.

———. "Native American Indian Literature: Critical Metaphors of the Ghost Dance." *World Literature Today,* 223–27, Vol. 66, No. 1, winter 1992.

CHAPTER FOUR

Coyote, Contingency, and Community: Thomas King's *Green Grass, Running Water* and Postmodern Trickster

[T]rickster stories point to the way ordinary, conventional reality is an illusory construction produced out of a particular univocal interpretation of phenomena appearing as signs. This deeper wisdom about the linguisticality of our constructed world and the illusoriness of that construction is where trickster stories open onto the sacred.
—Anne Doueihi, "Inhabiting the Space"

"It's still weird though," said Minnie. "Who would want to kill John Wayne?"
"Hmmmm," says Coyote, "all this floating imagery must mean something."
"That's the way it happens in oral stories," I says.
—Thomas King, *Green Grass, Running Water*

Old Ones

AMONG THE NUMEROUS chimerical developments to occur in Thomas King's *Green Grass, Running Water* (1993), perhaps the most telling occurs as the four old Indians alter the outcome of the allegedly famous John Wayne western *The Mysterious Warrior*. Having traipsed from a Florida hospital to the Blackfoot reserve in Canada, the four hundred-year-old Indians have set out in an effort to "change the world." Reckoning that the "classic" movie is as good a place as any to start, the old ones stealthily alter the "well-known" final scene of the movie as it unfolds on the immense video wall of Wild Bill Bursum's home entertainment center. While the assembled watch, John Wayne and his co-star Richard Widmark suffer cinematic deaths usually reserved for Indians. Appearing vanquished, cornered in Monument Valley, the Indians who had been pursued by the cavalry for the entire movie "began to shoot back, and soldiers began falling over. Sometimes two or three soldiers would drop at once, clutching their chests or their stomachs. . . . John Wayne looked down and stared stupidly at the arrow in his thigh, shaking his head in amazement and disbelief as two bullets ripped through his chest and out the back of his jacket. Richard Widmark collapsed face down in the sand, his hands clutching at an arrow buried in his throat" (284). Present among witnesses to this magic event, besides the four old Indians—Eli,[1] his nephew Lionel,[2] Charley Looking Bear,[3] and the hapless Bursum—is trickster Coyote,[4] whose gleeful response is a resounding "Yahoo!" (284).

Indeed, the moment is telling for it delightfully alludes to the ways in which King's Coyote intervenes at the level of perception, and challenges us to conceive of new, even audacious possibilities. Coyote's "Yahoo" signals the subversive reversal of the culturally resonant image of John Wayne felling Indians. New stories emerge in the process; old stories change. In a similar way, Coyote and the four old ones mischievously subvert and entangle a variety of other stories in *Green Grass*—stories ultimately bound up in the cultural processes of signification and representation itself.

From this perspective, King's Coyote can be viewed as intervening in the semiotic realm—a realm where cultural signifiers and politicized discursive structures produce meaning and coherent stories. King's Coyote thus exemplifies a "semiotic trickster," a version of what Gerald Vizenor has termed a "comic holotrope." As a comically disruptive sign, Coyote forces us to consider how interpretations and "readings" of the world are ceaselessly influenced by issues related to colonial representation and power, and how meaning and significance can mutate when conventional categories of perceptions shift. Such a liberative lesson ultimately serves to help heal King's protagonist Lionel, as well as other members of his contemporary Blackfoot community, allowing them to see new life possibilities. A "semiotic trickster," Vizenor emphasizes, "is a healer and comic liberator . . . not an artifact or real victim in oral summaries . . . [but] a communal sign in imagination . . . that endures in modern [Native American] literature" ("Trickster" 204).

It is precisely this "semiotic trickster"—a disjunctive, disruptive, and potentially radically subversive trickster—that runs through King's *Green Grass* and influences its slippery narrative strategies with themes of resistance and liberation. Correspondingly, King's Coyote emerges, not so much as a representative of anthropomorphic, embodied versions of trickster, but rather as a linguistic construct sent forth to disrupt our acceptance of certain "old stories"—stories that collude in the oppression of Native Americans. King's postmodern Coyote, as such, elucidates important contemporary interpretations of orality itself, as well as current poststructuralist discussions of culture, history, and anthropology. As James Clifford reminds us, "even the simplest cultural accounts are intentional creations" (10). In turn, we, as readers confronting King's beguiling narrative, are collectively redefined and transfigured into alternative communities made aware of the political nature of representation and all "cultural accounts." Rather than entering into word games, or even into communities structured by shared interpretation, we are absorbed into a narrative play wherein the oral moment of the story necessarily displaces any "fixed" interpretive structure.[5] We decode narrative and apprehend meaning in other ways; and, through this acquired apprehension, our relationships with Others and with the text shift. Older hierarchies and simplistic understandings fracture, providing not only other ways to read, but through these readings, new ways of seeing the world.

Postmodern Tricksters

Until recently, the image of Native American tricksters as embodied beings has been a persistent fantasy within the social imaginary of the West. Indeed, traditional religious and anthropological interpretations of trickster have tended to construct trickster as a comic *figure*, who assumes human or animal poses. Paul Radin's seminal study of Winnebego trickster cycles, for example, presents trickster as an individual neither "human being [n]or god, but something of both" (35). As an embodied isolate, Radin's trickster functions within traditional stories at the level of character, and, in turn, his operations may be regarded as metaphorical. Recently, William Bright has described trickster as a mythic figure, who, though a giver of fire, was also a "gross lecher and inevitable thief, liar, outlaw, a prankster whose schemes regularly backfire" (3).

In emphasizing the human aspects of such figures as Old Man Coyote, Bright asserts that, in "the Native American context, [tricksters] are not animals; they are first people . . . , members of a race of mythic prototypes who lived before humans existed. . . . They had tremendous powers . . . and were also capable of being brave or cowardly, conservative or innovative, wise or stupid" (xi). Such anthropomorphic descriptions have invariably lead to a kind of typology, founded on seeing trickster as a mythical being: trickster is thus a *figure* whose disparate and contradictory traits include liar, truth-teller, giver, thief, conservative, transgressor, wise, fool, lecher, or innocent.

Recent critical commentaries informed by a poststructuralist vocabulary, however, have begun to assail this anthropomorphic version of trickster, viewing it in part as emblematic of a western humanistic desire to embody trickster in a humanizing rhetoric of presence. Perhaps most vocal in this regard has been Gerald Vizenor, who reads such constructions of tricksters as illustrative of the "monologic" quality of western anthropology, and its persistent desire to construct "Indian" within limited parameters. For Vizenor, humanistic anthropomorphic versions of trickster—as fully embodied—erode what he argues is the tropic, semiotic function of trickster. In his own trickster tales Vizenor vigorously resists notions of a mythic trickster—a trickster who transcends language—firmly rooting his tricksters within entanglements of discourse. Concurrently, Vizenor finds a resonant vocabulary for describing the semiotic workings of trickster within the terms of poststructuralist thought and discourse. Asserting that "semiotic theories reveal more about trickster narratives (the texture of language and structure of sentences) than do theories of social science" (*Chance* 189), Vizenor argues that trickster as "comic holotrope"—as a nexus of signs, enjoining the speaker/writer with interpretive community—functions at the level of language and representation:

Tropes are figures of speech; here the trickster is a sign that becomes a comic holotrope, a consonance of sentences in various voices, ironies, variations in cultural myths and social metaphors. Comic holotropes comprise signifiers, the signified, and signs, which in new critical theories provided a discourse on the trickster in oral narratives, translations and modern imaginative literature. (190)

Indeed, Vizenor's own postmodern trickster tales, like King's *Green Grass*, represent highly imaginative efforts to remake and reinscribe the sacred trickster within the postmodern context. *Darkness in St. Louis Bearheart*, with its multivalent levels of narrative, comic playfulness, deconstructive thrusts, and overall critique of Western notions of stable truths, might very well be considered the archetypal trickster narrative of modern imaginative literature. Trickster's influence in *Bearheart*, as in Vizenor's later stories and novels *Heirs of Columbus* and *An American Monkey King in China*, forces readers to listen to trickster, to challenge their preconceptions regarding Western notions of "history," "reality," and the "sacred." As Alan Velie notes, Vizenor accomplishes this through his own "trick," getting readers to see the world through trickster eyes. "Vizenor writes like a trickster," states Velie, "creating a narrator who is a professed trickster, telling a story of tricksters, all with the purpose of turning the audience into tricksters" (136).

While such postmodern permutations of trickster may seem to detract from the figure's inherent sacredness, such constructions ironically offer a significant lesson in spiritual growth founded on new ways of seeing. Echoing Vizenor's desire to reinscribe trickster within the semiotic realm, Anne Doueihi argues that traditional Western religious and anthropological interpretations that depict a transcendent trickster have to do with a Western preoccupation with origins. Trickster is sacred, the logic of this narrative proceeds, and thus must be understood as an embodied figure whose origins exist beyond history. Thus by overlooking the complicated semiotic features of trickster stories, and by "taking narrative and meaning reverentially—as story and signified"—traditional scholarship has constructed a "parallel conception of trickster stories as themselves meaningful in that (and only that) they figure in the great story of human civilization, in the great story which is the history of religion" (194). As such, these constructions legitimize the notions of universality and hierarchy, placing the trickster within some larger Western narrative of an embodied, monotheistic form of spirituality.

By contrast, a poststructuralist interpretative paradigm allows Doueihi to view trickster stories as discursive constructs that "play" in the space between "discourse" and "story," between narrative structure and the act of telling a story. From this perspective, "story" is defined as "a sequence of actions or events, independent of their manifestation in discourse;" and "discourse" is "the discursive presentation of narration of events" (193). By overemphasizing the referential aspects of the "story" within trickster narratives, many interpreters often overlook the way the story's position within a complicated discursive web detracts from any fixed or transparent meaning. Such readings invariably lead to readings of trickster stories as mediums for referential, "univocal" interpretations of reality.

But by focusing on the semiotic structure of trickster stories, and how such a structure "performs" on the listener/reader of trickster narratives, we can begin to understand how such transparent, overreferential meanings unravel. Read from this vantage, trickster narratives undermine stable meanings and hold up such positivistic groundings as suspect, untrustworthy, and comically foolish. Thus, "[i]nstead of having one meaning, the text opens onto a plurality of meanings, none of which is exclusively 'correct,' because as the narrative develops in the trickster stories, the conventional level of meaning ceases to be appropriate" (199). For Douiehi, this semiotic lesson of trickster tales has liberatory power:

> It is the power of signification, the possibility to mean, that the trickster celebrates. . . . [I]n the trickster's world, everything is already a sign of something. It is a sign because it is part of a sacred world; it is a sign of the sacred. The universe is essentially linguistic and ultimately, infinitely interpretable. The trickster is thus not a sacred being, but the way the whole universe may become meaningful, sacred, and filled with "power." (201)

Blackfoot Coyote

In *Green Grass, Running Water,* it is just such a liberative journey, aided by Coyote, that the story both "performs" and thematizes in its depiction of a community of contemporary Blackfoot, who negotiate life on and off the reserve. Unlike King's first novel, *Medicine River* (1989), which deals with life on the Blackfoot Canadian reserve in a relatively straightforward and seemingly linear way, *Green Grass* as a postmodern trickster narrative shrouds its story with a dense discursive web that undermines any stable interpretive platform. Adopting a form of what Vizenor has called "mythic verism" (*Narrative*), *Green Grass* delights in interspersing the "fantastic" and implausible, with the all too real. Multistoried, multivoiced, playfully postmodern, *Green Grass* presents mutually informing stories that merge myth, history, tribal folklore, biblical scripture, myriad tribal and dominant culture referents—all of which circulate like running water within the shifting frame of King's trickster story.

Amid this polyvocality, two basic stories unfold—one magical, one "realistic." The "realistic" story has to do with Lionel and the daily lives of his Blackfoot friends and family as they head toward convergence at an annual sun dance[6] on the Blackfoot reserve in Canada. This central story concerns the individual struggles of Lionel's "academic" Uncle Eli, Lionel's feminist/teacher girlfriend Alberta, and Charlie Looking Bear, a lawyer. All except Lionel have left the reserve to seek lives on the "outside," and the sun dance marks a communal coming home. For Eli in particular, who has left academia, the sun dance emerges as a celebration of the traditional past, which leads to his occupation of an old family house, threatened by the building of a dam on Indian property. Ultimately it is Eli's influence— aided by Coyote—that causes Lionel to reconsider the value of stories and community elemental to native tradition.

The magically playful segments concern trickster Coyote, various "creation" stories, and the four old Indians who have left a Florida hospital to save Lionel. Like trickster Coyote, the four old Indians move back and forth between levels of narrative, playfully influencing the realistic aspects of the story. Eventually these levels of narrative merge, constructing the novel's complex and playful "mythic verism."

At the intersections of these levels of narrative, several textual conversations emerge. Although these dialogues are necessarily intertwined, identity, ethnicity, culture, and history develop as significant topics. Appropriately, in the space between these conversations stands King's trickster Coyote, whose movement across a range of conceptual borders problematizes ontological and epistemological interpretations of the world. Levels of narrative ceaselessly contaminate one another, stories ceaselessly modify each other, causing readers to continually "invent" the text, to suspend final interpretation within the indeterminate space of the interconnecting stories. In this way King's narrative compels readers to enter the complicated arena of trickster, to learn how language conditions reality and meaning among communal exchanges. This dialectical worldmaking is consistent with what Doueihi views as trickster's spiritual lesson: "The trickster shows us a way to see the world by opening our minds to the spontaneous transformations of a reality that is always open and creative. . . . It is in the language out of which they are constructed that trickster stories make accessible the deeper wisdom about the nature of the world" (200).

Ultimately, it is through this rupturing stable linguistic ground that *Green Grass* allows for the possibility of transformation, the acceptance of new stories and possibilities. Understood from this perspective, King's *Green Grass* theorizes itself, performatively "making readers into tricksters." It is "performative" in that it is an active text, a text that acts on the reader and requires new ways of seeing. This performativity ultimately lies at the center of King's story and is intricately tied to the novel's central lesson concerning Native American survival.

That *Green Grass* will attempt to provide this important lesson in cultural survival and renewal is signaled early on when Alberta has a discussion with her class that alludes to the ancient Indians, who will help Lionel come to a similar awareness. The old Indians' names are Crusoe,[7] Hawkeye,[8] Lone Ranger,[9] and Ishmael. Though mysterious at first, it is revealed soon that they are tribal representatives delivered to Florida at the end of the Indian wars—Cheyenne, Kiowa, Comanche, and Arapaho. Having escaped onto the road, they are out to "change the world," though how that will happen is at first uncertain. Like their sometime companion Coyote, they too travel between the "realistic" and mythic spaces of King's narrative. In their playful exchanges with each other, they incessantly tell their "own" stories of creation, each comically modifying events according to their individual traditions.

During Alberta's history lesson, it becomes evident that these Indians are somehow associated with the wayward Indians who had "painted their stories" after having been driven off their traditional lands and forcibly relocated to a Florida detention center at Fort Marion. As Alberta, a Blackfoot who has left the reserve and become a teacher, explains to her students: "In 1874, the U.S. army began a campaign of destruction aimed at forcing the southern Plains tribes into reservations. The army systematically went from village to village burning houses, killing horses, and destroying food supplies. They pursued the Cheyenne, Kiowa, Comanche, and the Arapaho relentlessly into one of the worst winters of the decade. Starvation and freezing conditions finally forced the tribes to surrender" (15). Alberta goes on to show her class "Plain's Indian Ledger Art," which she explains was drawn by some of the captive Indians, depicting such things as "the battles they had fought with the army and other tribes, "their life on the plains," and "life in prison" (16).[10]

But when Alberta asks what the students might deduce from the drawings and meets with silence, she asks: "Do they tell us anything about the people who did them or the world in which they lived?" Encountering more silence, she tells the students that none of the Indians escaped—but implies that the drawings themselves, spiritual and transportive in nature, suggest a kind of spiritual escape. This history lesson, shrouded in mystery, becomes important because it represents a lesson in cultural expectation, interpretation, and reading.

The "stories" drawn by the Indians cannot become intelligible to the students, because they don't possess the cultural or conceptual vocabulary to understand them. Moreover, the spirituality of the Indians cannot be discovered in the paintings, because the students lack the context from which they might recognize meaning. Only by understanding the "story" of Indian annihilation and erasure in America, might the story of spiritual survival and fortitude be grasped. In this sense, the students, like readers, need to break free from the hegemony of traditional "white" stories of the frontier, and begin to understand how history is a construct. Such wisdom could provide an interpretive space wherein ancient Indians hitchhiking across the continent might become a possibility. Only through learning to (re)read the past can Alberta's students reconstruct Native American history and, in doing so, reconstruct the Native American community.

Importantly, as a trickster "performance," the dialogic structure of *Green Grass* immediately foregrounds the linguistic and cultural processes that produce meaning, and which have crucial relevance to Alberta's lesson in reading and interpreting history. Readers literally enter *Green Grass* through an ongoing conversational gambit. The novel begins by invoking the mythic space of origin stories in the oral tradition:

> So.
> IN THE BEGINNING, THERE WAS NOTHING. JUST THE WATER.
> Coyote was there, but Coyote was asleep. That coyote was asleep and that Coyote was dreaming. When Coyote dreams, anything can happen.
> I can tell you that. (1)

Following this, however, a number of demystifying gestures occur, undermining the clear spirituality of this mythic space, and introducing parody. In particular, this dialogic panel is followed by other similar panels in which the four old Indians muse about how to begin the story. The quartet tries various openings, sounding in their comic banter much like Beckettian fools: "ONCE UPON A TIME"; "A LONG TIME AGO IN A FAR AWAY LAND"; "MANY MOONCOMECHUKA. . . . Hahahahahahahahaha . . ."; "IN THE BEGINNING GOD CREATED THE HEAVENS AND EARTH" (6–11).[11]

These playful exchanges, which emphasize various conventional discursive strategies for staging stories, correspondingly point to *Green Grass*'s staging of discursivity itself. Literary openings are attended by various codes, expectations, rules, logic(s), and their own ability to produce a conventional "sense of an ending." The old Indians finally try numerous variations, and in doing so, comically unmask the contingencies associated with storytelling, reality, and expectation.

Coyote shares this surfacing and resurfacing frame with the four old Indians. Here, trickster Coyote quite literally occupies the space between discourse and story. Functioning as Vizenor's mischievous and disruptive "comic holotrope," Coyote confuses the "simple" story of Lionel's attainment of wisdom, by constantly returning emphasis to *Green Grass* as a novel whose "moral" lesson will develop in part out of the text's trickster performance and beguiling structure. This decentering effect is again underscored in the curious conversation that opens the novel and precedes the "realistic" portion of the story concerned with Lionel's life. The exchange involves Coyote, Coyote's Dream, and "I":

Who are you? says that dream. Are you someone important?
"I'm Coyote," says Coyote. "And I am very smart."
I am very smart, too, says that dream. I must be Coyote.
"No, " says Coyote. "You can't be a Coyote. But you can be a dog."
When that Coyote dream thinks about being a dog, it gets everything mixed up. It gets everything backwards. (2)

Like a lens that distorts differently with each returning glance, this opening establishes the slippery semiotic games recurrent throughout *Green Grass*. "I" here clearly refers to King, the creative trickster who is constructing the narrative, but also to trickster as trope—as a signifier in narrative—as well as to a figure who speaks and seems embodied. "I" is also a character, who is involved in the story, a construction like trickster. Similarly, in this backwards story, dog is transformed into GOD, a God who is a signifier that cannot transcend, but who nonetheless promises to become "sacred" in this story of renewal.

Readers reading/interpreting through this disruptive lens, then, must always be aware that they are involved in constructing meaning rather than reading a linear or cohesive story. In this way, the novel engages readers in an active collaboration that has resonances with Michail Bakhtin's notion of "heteroglossia," a concept that underscores the semiotic contingencies that condition all aspects of "telling" and representation.

In *Keeping Slug Woman Alive*, Greg Sarris correspondingly engages Mikhail Bakhtin's notion of heteroglossia to underscore and emphasize how Native Pomo oral traditions—in many ways similar to Lionel's Blackfoot traditions—reflect similar masking and unmasking features within their sacred story traditions. For Sarris, such oral traditions emphasize the contingency of meaning and reality by self-consciously underscoring that worldviews are storied constructs. Using his sister's voice to make the point, he writes that for natives the "[t]hings you hear come back. A story for us Indians is like a cork in water. No matter where it goes, no matter how much you push, it floats back to the top" (11). Sarris further asserts: "[f]or us, a story or teaching is never complete. . . . A story's meaning is dependent on the life beyond it. . . . Words and stories poison the healthy, heal the sick, empower lovers, transform the world." (127)

Bakhtin's commentary on the dialogic influences on the novel and language thus provides a resonant way for Sarris to discuss the complexity informing oral culture and its emphasis on stories. Sarris concurs with Bakhtin, who notes that language is "heteroglot from top to bottom: it represents the coexistence of sociological contradictions between the present and the past, between the differing epochs of the past, between different socio-ideological groups in the present, between tendencies, schools, circles, and so forth, all given bodily form" (4). Correspondingly, in conversations with his family friend Mabel, Sarris notes a similar polyvocality: "Mabel provokes . . . a specific dialogue, or conversation, that can open the intermingling of multiple voices within and between people they encounter, enabling people to see and hear the way voices intersect and overlap, the ways that they have been repressed or held down because of certain social and political circumstances and the ways they can be talked about and usurped" (5). Thus, as Sarris's works elucidate, many native oral traditions, of which trickster is a part, are fundamentally self-conscious about the ways in which stories circulate within communities, the manner in which such tales gain meaning, and are thus always contingent.

Similarly, Brian McHale in *Postmodernist Fiction* invokes Bakhtin's model to discuss the way postmodern narratives foreground polyvocality to emphasize the political and ideological factors involved in the production of "worlds." Emphasizing this point, McHale cites Bakhtin:

Every language in the novel is a point of view, a socio-ideological conceptual system of real social groups and their embodied representatives. . . . [A]ny point of view on the world fundamental to the novel must be concrete, a socially embodied point of view, not an abstract, purely semantic position. . . . [And]. . . an actual social life and historical becoming create within an abstractly unitary national language a multitude of concrete worlds, a multitude of bounded verbal-ideological and social belief systems. (165)

For McHale, postmodern texts thus foreground the production of meaning, of "worlds." As he writes, "by heightening the polyphonic structure and sharpening the dialogue in various ways," postmodern fiction "foregrounds the ontological dimension for the confrontation among discourses, the achieving of a polyphony of worlds" (166).

In provocative ways, King's *Green Grass*—as a trickster narrative—marks the intersection between McHale's postmodernism and Sarris's native oral traditions. *Green Grass*'s performative strategies thus reveal and reverse, while collaborating with the reader in its dialogic structure, the "poisoning" power of words and stories. This critique is comically evident in *Green Grass*'s numerous playful references to words and names that refract their traditional placements within "white" narratives. Most obvious is the use of the names Ishmael, Defoe, Hawkeye, and the Lone Ranger. Here, these names refer to Indians—not the "white" halves of what Leslie Fielder long ago described as the frontier couple. "Uncoupled" from works that produced and grounded their former signification/identifications, the names playfully reveal the way the Other functions as an indelible component within discovery and frontier narratives, servicing the psycho-social construction of the Euro-American self. Similarly, numerous "historical" names and referents are detached from their traditional contexts, and float as signifiers throughout the text. Old names are fixed to new identities.

In the water world, the "realistic world," Henry Dawes is not a famous advocate of Indian Christianization and education, but an inquisitive child. Mary Rowlandson refers not to the famous captive, but to a school girl. Camelot is not a mythical place, but a "progressive" Indian hospital prone to "minor mistakes." Pocahantas is not a famous east-coast Indian, but a modern stripper, "the sexiest squaw west of the Mississippi" (186). Similarly, Adam, of biblical fame, has been recast as Ahdamn, and circulates within the mythic loop of creation stories that occur in the "skyworld." Here, too, Old Woman and grandmother Turtle, having slipped out of traditional space of Blackfoot stories, discuss microwave ovens and Ahdamn's penchant for naming everything in a "garden" that isn't really his in the first place.

In a zany way, King's unhinging and recasting of these names thus forces a "confrontation between discourses," which inevitably pushes us toward a recognition of how certain stories attain purchase within cultures. The traditional place for these names exists within matrices of discursive fields that are subtended with power relations. Of course, within the hegemonic productions of such ideas as "the frontier" and "Indian," many of these traditional sites of signification are associated with the tyranny and oppressiveness of colonial representations and production of meaning. In *Green Grass* this critique quite obviously leads to King's humorous play on the way we "read" our respective worlds, and the cultural tensions that exist between forms of discursive production. As a semiotic border crosser, King's Coyote moves "betwixt and between" these discourses too, revealing how discourse and stories quite literally produce certain versions of such constructs as "reality" and "history."

The lesson in reading/seeing that occurs throughout *Green Grass* is emblematic in the "who's on first" exchanges between the receptionist Babo— who is supposed to know about the old Indians—and the hapless detective Cereno, who has come to question her at the hospital. Babo and Cereno, of course, are familiar names from Herman Melville's famous trickster narrative *Benito Cereno*. As in Melville's story, Cereno is the victim of representation, caught between two "worlds." When Sergeant Cereno asks Babo about the escapees, she says "Well, they were old" (47). And when he presses further about their identity and background, she tells Cereno, "We used to talk, you know, life, kids, fixing the world. . . . We'd trade stories, too, the Indians and me. That's what I could do, you know, tell you one of the stories they told me" (47). Of course, Cereno can no more understand the stories of ancient Indians who walk the earth, than Alberta's students could understand the secret language of the Plains ledger art.

Repeatedly, in similar ways, characters in *Green Grass* find themselves captives of their own conceptual vocabularies and stories. Bill Bursom can only relate to Indians as figures in John Wayne movies. Charlie Looking Bear's father is fired from movies because his nose "is too big for an Indian." Latisha, Lionel's sister, is beaten by her husband because she doesn't conform to the image of an "Indian" wife. Eli is haunted by the memory of border guards who confiscated his father's sacred head-dress because, to them, it only represented a mass of "illegal" feathers.

As in Melville's *Benito Cereno*, all these readings of reality rely on culturally embedded perceptions—on grounding within in discursive fields. In *Green Grass*, as in Melville's story, water is the predominant metaphoric medium that signals worlds are afloat. Unlike Melville's Cereno, who knows that Babo's barber's knife at his throat can be "read" in painfully different ways, King's detective ultimately lacks the acquisition of such sacred knowledge. In Vizenor's words, he is doomed to his "terminal creeds," a form of epistemological production that disallows difference. He is simply unable to understand. Moreover, his captivity within narratives is reflexive with *Green Grass*'s larger interrogation of the way written "historical" narratives perpetuate the entrapment of native cultures within the "static" historical representations of the past. This process is exposed in King's depiction of the "three" mistakes that threaten to keep Lionel working at Bill Bursom's entertainment center.

In Lionel's case, his initial gloominess and feeling of alienation quite literally are precipitated by the unyielding narratives of his so-called past. The narrative that haunts Lionel began when he was a child, when he feigned tonsillitis, thinking he would get to stay home from the reservation school. But his plan goes awry, and he only narrowly averts a heart operation after a nurse confuses his identity. Long after the mishap, though, people assume Lionel "has a heart problem," and this assumption proves disruptive. Similarly, years later, while a student in college, he is asked to speak at a gathering of Indians. Though not really an activist, Lionel goes, and he soon finds himself in a stolen van heading toward the 1973 siege at

Wounded Knee. Pursued by police and later arrested while "carrying a gun," Lionel protests that he doesn't really "know a thing about AIM" (American Indian Movement) (56). But even after the charges are dropped, a cop tells him: "Get your life together. With your record, you're running out of options" (56). Of course, with a "heart condition," and being a dangerous, gun-carrying member of AIM, Lionel can only get a job at Bill Bursum's home entertainment center just beyond the reserve—his third mistake.

King's presentation of Lionel's life as a life seemingly without options, as prefigured by fictions that proceed him but which nonetheless conspire to fix his identity and delimit possibility, allegorizes the familiar historic process of domination of Native Americans by written colonial narratives and "official histories," which have historically served to "invent" what it means to be an Indian. And such written histories obviously serve as oppresive and destructive colonial corollaries to the "actual" material violence and dispossession experienced by indigenous cultures. Often, historically, within such written histories, Indians emerge as a collective, a static "sign" themselves, imprisoned a "tragic" but necessary narrative of decline and ultimate erasure. Lionel's liberation from his own "written histories," fittingly comes from the power of spoken stories. Indeed, Coyote asserts the power of orality to resist such fixed narratives, to voice new forms of liberation.

In *The Writing of History*, postmodern theorist Michel de Certeau has asserted that it is the "native voice" that the colonial writing of history has traditionally repressed or omitted, but which potentially has the power to disrupt written history in the West. For de Certeau, the production of history within the colonial context, and its "heteronomous variants"—ethnology, pedagogy—have been predicated on "leaving" the native voices behind. Contrasting orality with the sovereignty of written inscriptions of history and ethnology, he suggests that the writing of history occurs only when the "voice" of the other is repressed, for it cannot possibly be contained. Rather, the speech of the other must be exiled from historical and ethnological reportage, made "exotic," for it is precisely that which holds the potential to destabalize the "continuity of signs" desired by such accounts.

Writing thus "produces history" as an "archive" whose "will to power is invested in its form" (215–17), and whose mission is the "manufacture of time and reason" (226). The voice of the other thus comes to represent that which "cannot be put into words," that which would signal a "rift," a "jump" in the religio-historic production of meaning (230–32). Similarly, Homi Bhabha stresses the importance of orality as a mode of resistance to written colonial narratives. Orality, suggests Bhabha, resists hegemony and encourages more "hybrid," and communal worldviews. As such, orality itself is "enunciative." As Bhabha explains, "the enunciative is a more dialogic process that attempts to track displacements and realignments that are the effects of cultural antagonisms—and articulations—subverting the rationale of the hegemonic moment and relocating alternative, hybrid sites of cultural negations" (443).

In *Green Grass*, voice and the oral traditions, of which Coyote is a prominent part, prove central as a liberating mode of resistance. Orality—the spoken story with its momentary presence—subverts the fixed narrative of any written tale. Spoken stories insist upon a narrative dynamism rather than codifying a static representation. Orality indeed displaces absence with an active, disruptive, and fleeting presence; it undermines the encoded narrative, which seeks to contain Native American discourse. For King's Blackfoot community, stories voiced among friends thus hold the potential to intervene in a powerful way in the "the writing" of their lives, and in particular Lionel's.

Fittingly, it is amid a cacophony of competing transcultural and intertextual voices in King's story that Lionel's story of liberation emerges. As might be expected, the moment of Coyote's interventions and Lionel's renewal occurs when Eli takes Lionel to the annual sun dance at the reserve. The sun dance is a sacred rite of transformation—of revision. And the sun dance is communal, a shared experience celebrating the plurality of voices of its participants.

Prior to his return to the reserve and participation in the sun dance, Eli too, like Lionel, suffers from the prohibitions associated with his identity within the dominant culture. He too feels the pressure of "fixed narratives." Having left the reserve and earned a Ph.D. in literature, his path seemed predestined by cultural expectations, based on old stories without possibility of revision. He had become the "Indian who couldn't go home" (253):

It was a common enough theme in novels and movies. Indian leaves the traditional world of the reserve, goes to the city, and is destroyed. Indian leaves the traditional world of the reserve, is exposed to white culture, and becomes trapped between two worlds. Indian leaves the traditional world of the reserve, gets an education, and is shunned by his tribe.
Indians. Indians. Indians.
Ten little Indians. (253)

Correspondingly, Eli's own story of renewal—his acquired ability to imagine different possibilities in a once seemingly circumscribed future—is revealed through a series of stories that hold the key to his emancipation. And it is in the passing on of these stories to Lionel that he hopes to offer him a lesson, a way to change his life.

This lesson occurs on the way to the sun dance, in which Lionel has reluctantly accompanied Eli. As they ride in a car toward the site of the annual sun dance, Eli begins to try and explain his motives for returning home, hoping it will have some resonance for Lionel. First, Eli tells the story of his wife Karen's death, and her desire to see the sun dance before she died. Having suffered "incurable cancer," and then survived, Karen goes back with Eli to his "home" to watch the sun dance. Eli explains that, off the reservation, "everything was new" (320), but that returning to see the sun dance had been important. Later, Karen is killed by a drunk driver in a seemingly meaningless accident. As Eli tells the story, Lionel asks about returning home to the see the sun dance: "Change your life?" And Eli responds, "No," "Can't say it did. . . . Can't just tell you that straight out. Wouldn't make any sense. Wouldn't be much of a story" (320).

Eli's point is clear; telling the story requires other stories, perhaps even stories that go beyond him. He explains: "After [Karen] died, I thought about coming home. . . . But I didn't" (320). Again he pauses, unable to construct his story in a way that will convey what it is he is trying to tell Lionel. Presently, the road they drive along toward the more expansive reaches of the reservation begins to open up. Possibility looms, but also brings fear:

The road ran on in front of them, a pitch of hills and coulees that dipped and rose on the land. It had been a long time since Lionel had travelled the lease road. Normally, he came in through Fort McLeode on the road that ran to Cardston. That road was all asphalt and mileage signs and billboards. The road was a wild thing, bounding across the prairies, snaking sideways, and, each crest of the hill, the road would vanish, and they would tumble out into the tall grass and disappear. (321)

Along the vanishing road, disappearance becomes as possible as emergence. Here, Eli again searches for the right way to explain his return. But as he does so, the car gains the crest, exposing the encampment of the Blackfoot sun dance ceremony. The image proves resonant: "Below in the distance, a great circle of tepees floated on the prairies, looking for the world like sailing ships adrift on the ocean." At this point Eli turns to Lionel and puts his answer in the form of a question: "What about it, nephew? Where would you want to go?" (321).

Eli's answer as to why he came home is thus not really an answer at all. Rather, for Lionel as well as readers, it becomes a kind of wise trickster

riddle, a narrative that escapes total meaning except as a temporary assigna-
tion within involutions of other narratives. As the watery image suggests,
meaning shifts, contexts float. Nonetheless, the lesson is important: it is
clear that the telling of stories, as well as Lionel's understanding that Blackfoot culture is dependent upon his own telling of stories is the important
lesson here. Eli's question signals the importance of conversation, the necessity of Lionel's response and his part in a communal construction of
meaning.

Later this lesson gets underscored at the sun dance itself, where Coyote
and the four old Indians join Eli and Lionel. Trickster's entrance into the
narrative sequence is consonant with transformation, with ruptures both
semiotic and psychic. This anxiety regarding renewal and the rebirth of
possibility becomes evident when Eli, in the company of his family, gets
into an argument with George, Latisha's white husband who derides the
ceremony. "You can't believe that shit," George tells Eli, who prepares to
dance." This is ice-age crap. . . . Come on! It's the twentieth century. Nobody cares about your little powwow. A bunch of old people and drunks sitting around in tents in the middle of nowhere" (342). But, rather than Eli
being the one to respond to George, Lionel joins in, telling him: "There's
nothing for you here" (342). Lionel's response, of course, is the only thing
Coyote and the four old Indians need to hear. Though they tell Lionel that
"that's as much as we can do for you," he remains baffled. "That's it?" is all
he can say. Then Robinson Crusoe explains: "In the years that come . . .
you'll be able to tell our children and grandchildren about this." The men
then begin to dance, and the image of the camp as a renewed community
becomes resonant with the promise of Eli and Lionel's vision as they approached earlier by car: "The circle was tightly formed now, the older people sitting in the lawn chairs along the front edge, the younger people
standing in the back, the children constantly in motion. . . . In a while the
dancers would return to the centre lodge and the families would go back to
their tepees and tents. And in the morning, when the sun came out of the
east, it would begin again" (343). Lionel's healing lesson, facilitated by
trickster's intervention, concerns the value of community and stories in imagining new possibilities for tradition.

As might be expected, the final images of the novel return to the notion
of radical (un)grounding. Coyote's mischief produces an inadvertent earth-
quake, literally causing the ground to move, ultimately leading to Eli's
death by water as he occupies his mother's old house in the basin of the illegal parliament dam. Rather than becoming part of a "tragic narrative,"

however, his death is recontextualized and becomes instead an occasion for celebration. Subsumed by the deluge, he returns to the flowing water, the shifting space of eternal movement, change and renewal—"Below, in the valley, the water rolled on as it had for eternity" (356). And like the cabin, the family house symbolic of tradition remains but a trace in memory, though alive in stories. Months later, standing where both Eli and the house had once been, in the sliding mud and running water, Lionel's aunt Norma tells him: "I hope you took notes" (373). Then, "Eli's fine, he came home" (374). Lionel responds by saying "Yeah, . . . but he didn't come home because of the Sun Dance. And he didn't come home because Granny died. He told me that" (374).

Ultimately, Lionel never articulates why Eli had returned home; it is left as a shared secret, a story within a story. And in the same way, Lionel's quest for answers and identity is never resolved. "No truth but in stories," maintains King's character "I," and it is this truth that Lionel finally grasps. As readers we share in this secret, but we also must regard Lionel and Eli's story within the context of a trickster story, which seemingly always requires new acts of reading and interpretation. In King's fiction, Coyote calls, cars float away, John Wayne dies, and history changes, and through these fractured, seemingly impossible occasions a young Blackfoot man experiences renewal and the reader escapes the constructs of culture.

When King's story finally ends, it resists closure, suggesting the possibility of new stories. Coyote and "I" once again begin to "discuss how it happened." Implicitly, readers are invited to construct their own meaning, to enter into liberative conversation with Coyote. As readers of a "performative" postmodern trickster tale, we are indeed invited to participate, to join in the subversive potential of Coyote. Old stories change; new stories emerge.

At the conclusion of King's novel we are thus reminded of trickster's sacred function within traditional oral cultures as a healer, but also as a disruptive semiotic element that resists colonial representations and stories of containment. King's conclusion too reminds us that many Native American postmodern trickster stories have a political and cultural agenda; they encourage us to become members of a community engaged in telling, hearing, retelling, contradicting, and reweaving, rather than simply receiving. We, like King's protagonist Lionel, are thus beckoned by Coyote to see the world differently, to imagine new stories. Coyote's subversive "Yahoo" signals this liberative potential.

Notes

1. Eli is, at least on one level, a reference to the Old Testament prophets. Like those for whom he was named, Eli is a wise man whose experiences and prophesy will prefigure other later narratives, in the same way that the Old Testament prefigures the New. Eli here, too, clearly makes reference intertextually to Louise Erdrich's character who appears in her tetralogy, which includes *Love Medicine* and *The Bingo Palace*. See "Disruptive Genealogies" in this volume. This intertextual reference by King to other Native American texts typifies a range of references that move readers into other imaginative Native American landscapes.

2. Again, Lionel's name references at least several literary figures. Most obviously, he recalls the Lionel involved with the knights of the round table and their search for the holy grail. Because of his insistence upon finding meaning, his involvement in literary discussions with Eli, and his "liberal" notion that meaning will help create a better world, he is also easily associated with critic Lionel Trilling.

3. Charley Looking Bear's father's "origins" can be traced to the historical personage of Luther Standing Bear. Luther Standing Bear witnessed the Sand Creek Massacre, and later traveled with Buffalo Bill's wild west show. He played a political role in the final days of the Indian wars. Ultimately he moved to Hollywood where he played minor parts in early westerns. Luther Standing Bear's position in Native American history is uncertain; some see him as a successful "trickster," while others believe that he allowed himself to be appropriated by the white man.

4. Within traditional Blackfoot cosmology, trickster Coyote is called A-pe'si. Coyote is present at creation, during which he helps the Old Man (Na'pe) create the world, as well as men and women, from bones and buffalo. As with other Native American trickster figures, Blackfoot Coyote's interventions are alternately disruptive and constructive. In a number of traditional tales, A-pe'si refers to Na'pe as "brother," suggesting the significance of their interrelationship within oral creation stories. For an oral retelling of traditional Blackfoot stories, see Francis Frazer's *The Bear Who Stole the Chinook* (Vancouver: Douglas Press, 1991).

5. Quite evidently, much of poststructuralist and postmodern theory attempts to define "conventional western reception of texts," and to suggest that reading is always more about dislocation than a single unified and essential act of interpretation. Barthes, Derrida, Lyotard, and Bakhtin all have much to say that is relevant to the discussion here. Stanley Fish attempts to resolve the issue through his discussion of "interpretive communities." However, *Green Grass* deviates from these discussions in several important aspects. As a novel, it "theorizes" itself, rather than becoming the repository/subject or object of theoretical discussion. More importantly, as a trickster narrative, the novel marks the reader's necessary ability to re-create the text, rather than denoting the ways in which the text fractures and re-creates itself. For King, and for trickster fictions in general, the individual and orality function as a subtextualized counter-narrative to written textuality.

6. The discussions of the sun dance here also reference other religious celebrations associated with the sun. The sun also recalls, within the context of King's narrative, the Sun King and ultimately comments on Western hierarchies and appropriations. King indeed appears in his own narrative. Like Hitchcock, he references himself in his own cinema, of which he is indeed "king."

7. See, of course, *Robinson Crusoe*. Robinson Crusoe defined himself through his relationship with Friday. Crusoe comments at length upon the perfection of Friday,

noting his physical beauty and his essential goodness of character. This ideal construction contrasts with Crusoe's depiction of himself.

8. Hawkeye is one of the names for James Fenimore Cooper's Natty Bumppo. Like Crusoe, Hawkeye's identity is defined through his relationship with the "Other." And, like Crusoe, Hawkeye can be read as a place of origin for questing characters and for protagonists in the literature of discovery. Hawkeye provides a kind of paradigmatic figuration of this type in American fiction.

9. The Lone Ranger is an interesting presence. Like Hawkeye, he figures in a large number of tales, always accompanied by his "Other," Tonto. But the Lone Ranger is masked; his identity is obscured. He is a crusader of unknown origins. Like all the four hundred-year-old Indians, the Lone Ranger appropriates a name associated with imperialism, as a way of reclaiming identity.

10. Alberta's lessons are curiously reminiscent of the legendary Sequoyah. According to legend, Sequoyah believed that Native Americans would never have sufficient power to resist the Anglo incursion until they possessed writing. Sequoyah then devoted himself to the creation of a pictograph alphabet, and to the teaching of writing. Alberta's efforts to teach history through pictographs raises many of these same issues. Her place in King's narrative underlines the tension and incompatibility between oral story and written history.

11. King plays with a variety of creation stories in his text, perhaps in an attempt to note the very absurdity of these discussions of origins. The text transforms the nearly clichéd lines into Dadaist play. Coyote's lines, "In the beginning, there nothing. Just the water," conflict with the western notion of origin, which is expressed in terms of written language. "In the beginning there was the word," insists Western epistemology, arguing for an origin that began in fixed narrative. But Coyote's place in a narrative awash in moving water suggests a more mutable, dynamic story of origins.

Works Cited

Bhabha, Homi. "Post Colonial Criticism," *Remaking the Boundaries*. New York: Modern Language Association, 1993.

Bright, William. *A Coyote Reader*. Berkeley: University of California, Berkeley Press, 1993.

Clifford, James. *Writing Culture: The Poetics and Politics of Ethnography*. eds. J. Clifford and George E. Marcus. Berkeley: University of California Press, 1986.

de Certeau, Michel. *The Writing of History*. New York: Columbia University Press, 1988.

Doueihi, Anne. "Inhabiting the Space between Discourse and Story in Trickster Narratives," *Mythical Trickster Figures: Contours, Contexts and Criticisms*, eds. W. Hynes and W. Doty. Tuscaloosa: University of Alabama Press, 1993.

King, Thomas. *Medicine River*. Toronto: Penguin Books, 1989.

———. *All My Relations: An Anthology of Contemporary Canadian Native Fiction*. Norman: University of Oklahoma Press, 1992.

———. *Green Grass, Running Water*. Boston: Houghton Mifflin, 1993.

McHale, Brian. *Postmodernist Fiction*. London: Routledge, 1989.

———. *Constructing Postmodernism*. London: Routlege, 1992.

Melville, Herman. *Benito Cereno: Great Short Works of Herman Melville*, ed. Warner Berthoff. New York: Harper and Row, 1969.

Radin, Paul. *The Trickster.* New York: Schocken Books, 1972.
Sarris, Greg. *Keeping Slug Woman Alive.* Berkeley: University of California Press, 1994.
Velie, Alan. "The Trickster Novel," *Narrative Chance*, ed. Gerald Vizenor. Albuquerque: University of New Mexico Press, 1989.
Vizenor, Gerald. *Darkness in Saint Louis Bearheart.* St. Paul: Bookslinger, 1978.
———. "Bone Courts: The Rights and Narrative Representation of Tribal Bones." *American Indian Quarterly* 10 (1986): 319–32.
———. *Griever, An American Monkey King in China: A Novel.* New York: Fiction Collective, 1987.
———. *Narrative Chance: Postmodern Discourse of Native American Indian Literatures.* Albuquerque: University of New Mexico Press, 1989.
———. *Heirs of Columbus.* Hanover: Wesleyan University Press, 1991.
———. *Landfill Meditation: Crossblood Stories.* Hanover: Wesleyan University Press, 1991.
———. *Narrative Chance: Postmodern Discourse on Native American Indian Literatures.* Albuquerque: University of New Mexico Press, 1989.

CHAPTER FIVE

Displaced Horizons: Sergio Leone's Man With No Name; Films and the Politics of Postmodern Representation

> When I look at John Wayne's face I see everything. When I look at Clint Eastwood's face I see nothing.   —Sergio Leone

> I reckon he picked the wrong trail. Maybe he picked the wrong town. Maybe he should never have been born.   —*A Fistful of Dollars*

Fragmented Frontiers

THE SPAGHETTI WESTERN—that mock-heroic Italian sojourn into the territory of the frontier genre—is nearly synonymous with the 1960s film work of director Sergio Leone. While numerous other westerns had already been produced in Italy before Leone launched his Dollars trilogy, most notably by directors Sergio Corbucci, Sergio Sollima, and Damiani Valerii, Leone brought international recognition to the cinematic form.[1] Through Leone's satiric and even campy direction, the spaghetti western became emblematic of the coded violence inherent in frontier stories and also introduced a subversive, deconstructive element.

Leone's vastly popular films were largely condemned by film critics and intellectuals for their superficiality, their gratuitous violence, their absurd plot lines, and their vacant escapism. His work was panned by the *New Yorker* and dismissed as shallow "opportunism" (Landy 49). But while numerous critics remarked negatively on Leone's films, viewing them as a nadir point in culture, the movies broke attendance records in both the United States and in Europe. Leone's work proved to be hugely profitable and made Clint Eastwood a star.

The popular fervor that greeted Leone's films suggests that their appeal was not based solely on cheap escapism and empty machismo. Indeed, the popularity of the films, coupled with the psychic dislocations of the 1960s, makes it plausible to assume that the films also tapped the era's cultural anxieties, performing a kind of cultural work. Through a radical repositioning of the genre of the western, Leone's westerns examined the realignment and shifts that were restructuring American politics. The protracted national trauma of Vietnam, the Cuban missile crisis and the Bay of Pigs disaster, the reverberations associated with Sputnik and Gary Powers's aerial misadventure in his U-2, all find a coded representation within Leone's discourse.

Commenting on the development of the spaghetti western, as well as on nearly all the films of the 1960s—the popular "historical" dramas, as well as the "serious" works of Jean-Luc Godard and Akira Kurosawa—film critic Marcia Landy maintains that all these films reflected the anxiety of their cultural moment: "it is possible to see in these films shared antagonisms toward prevailing power structures, a concern with militarism and its deleterious effects, and a mistrust of state structures. . . . These films represent the crisis of cultural representation that was taking place on a worldwide scale" (Landy 45). The larger "crisis of representation" to which Landy alludes has concerned cultural critics as they examine both Leone's work and the culture of postmodernism itself.

The issues that surround Leone's westerns, and in particular his Eastwood trilogy of *A Fistful of Dollars* (1964), *For a Few Dollars More* (1965), and *The Good, the Bad and the Ugly* (1966) frame the debate that today concerns postmodernism and contemporary popular culture. The evident superficiality and banal violence of the films, as well as their exploration of the cultural and political climate of the 1960s, make them resonant with the current critical interrogation of the society of the millennium. What Fredric Jameson, in his seminal "The Cultural Logic of Late Capitalism," has termed "subjective schizophrenia" and a general lack of depth is interpreted by other critics as *jouissance* and liberation. It is in the space between these view points that Leone's texts play, for they are overtly, aggressively shallow; they simultaneously play with masculinity, the heroic, the notion of expansionism, and they mimic the social anxiety of the era. Prescient, Leone's work ushers in the self-reflexive, deconstructive terrain of the contemporary western.

Fredric Jameson's well-documented critique of postmodernism focuses frequently on visual or popular culture and argues that nothing new is produced by the era. Rather, the old enfeebled thought of modernism is recycled in a fragmented and entirely superficial and empty manner. For Jameson, popular culture today signals the "death of the imagination" and the failure of any culture outside the society of excess and spectacle. It is the culture of "blank parody"—a parody that mimics earlier forms and genres but does so reflexively without philosophical direction. Replicating earlier works, blank parody is not fueled by satiric impulse but is instead simply empty repetition. It is parody by the unenlightened and the unconscious. Its point is simply that there is no point. The "thematics of mechanical reproduction" have created a culture wherein television with its empty sit-coms and endless reruns of old movies has become, for Jameson, the era's central metaphor. This television metaphor—with its cops-and-robbers and cowboys-and-Indians plots—has created a cultural narrative of paranoia and easy conspiracy.[2] Quite clearly, Leone's films deliberately reflect both this "blankness" and "depthlessness." His plot lines reproduce the narratives of earlier westerns and their predictable conclusions, as well as the anxieties of the epoch. Leone's work contains all the primary elements of the frontier story. Yet these elements are decontextualized, disturbed, and so they simply saturate the viewer with their violent absurdity.

While undoubtedly accurate, Jameson's assessment is often resisted by critics more sympathetic to the postmodern sensibility. Jean-François Lyotard maintains that postmodernism, rather than being a dismal continuation of modernism, represents an epistemological shift. This shift is characterized by play, by the collapse of a unified vision to disparate horizons, by a liberating plurality, and by the privileging of information. From Lyotard's point of view, this is all to the good, and he sees Jameson's high-tech metaphor as producing and transforming endless arrangements of knowledge. This knowledge will imperil hegemony (Lyotard, *The Postmodern Condition*, 5–7).

Angela McRobbie, in her text, *Postmodernism and Popular Culture*, makes a point that is similar to Lyotard's. She too contends that play and repetitive transformation are political, for they subvert hegemonic discourse. Insists McRobbie: "the superficial does not necessarily represent a decline into meaninglessness or valuelessness in culture. . . . [T]he glossy surface of pop, the intertextual referencing between film and television . . . need not be seen as heralding the death of politics in culture, but it does mean that we need to develop a critical vocabulary which can take this rapid movement into account. . . . [T]he superficial can be a deliberate political strategy" (McRobbie 4). For McRobbie, the superficial becomes a deliberate space from which to disrupt homogeneous culture, making popular culture a political platform. McRobbie's argument provides a lens through which we can read Leone's work. *A Fistful of Dollars, For a Few Dollars More*, and *The Good, the Bad and the Ugly* represent Leone's attempt to develop a critical vocabulary, and in their exploration of politics, race, and masculinity the films become both consciously subversive and supremely superficial. In order to consider this cultural context, we need to consider the films against the bewildering tableau of 1960s Americana.

The Cold War and the Politics of Suspicion

On May Day of 1960, airman Gary Powers, piloting a U-2 aircraft over the Soviet Union, was shot down. Powers was subsequently captured, imprisoned, and, allegedly, tortured. In the wake of the fear and consternation that followed the incident, an unsettling truth emerged: the United States had been involved in unconfessed and possibly illegal espionage activities. The U-2, which American officials insisted was a weather-surveying craft flying routine missions over Turkey, was revealed to be a spy plane flying reconnaissance missions over the Soviet Union. The *New York Times* reported that, "because the intelligence activities of the United States have been discussed so little, there is widespread illusion that only the Communists resort to the black arts of diplomacy."[3]

Responding to the confusion of a naive public, Senator Clifford Case explained to his bewildered constituency, "It isn't a question of right. It is a question of what has to be done . . . to get all the possible information." The desirability of "information" was apparent to the public, because shortly before, the Russian spacecraft Sputnik had become airborne, signifying Soviet supremacy in the space race. Months later, the disastrous invasion attempt would take place at Cuba's Bay of Pigs.

In October of 1962, the installation of Soviet-made missiles on the island of Cuba was brought to the attention of the American public. A grave President Kennedy announced that this installation could only be regarded as the Soviet Union "raising its armed fist.[4] This troubling news was exacerbated by the insistence of some politicians that the CIA had provided photos of missiles in Cuba during the previous summer, and that JFK had delayed making any pronouncement in the hope that a more dramatic display of "brinkmanship" would increase his popularity. During this same autumn, Kennedy announced his intention of sending American troops into Vietnam as a necessary gesture to secure political stability.

But, a little over a year later, Kennedy was dead, and the nation was awash in diverse conspiracy theories. The average American was deeply troubled, both by what was apparent, and perhaps even more by the unknown questions yet to be posed. There were conspiracy theories but no demonstrable conspirators. The American populace could only sit back and watch the race riots that were beginning to appear on television, and contemplate the increased number of fall-out shelters. It was into this cultural milieu that Sergio Leone introduced his films, subverting the hegemony that had traditionally structured American westerns.

A Fistful of Dollars

Leone began work on *A Fistful of Dollars* in 1963, releasing the film in 1964. While the film did not emerge as a fully developed counter-western as later cinematic segments in the trilogy would, *Fistful* reflected the intensely anxious political climate, investigated the issues of race that had historically anchored the western, and began to develop an antihero who would question the patriarchal doctrines of the terrain.

The familiar tropes of the western—the hero, the villain, a frightened woman, a saloon, and a shootout—still remain. Yet the movie satirizes and redefines these images. Moreover, the film's protagonist, the Man With No Name, is an ineffectual hero, a bounty hunter and an amoral mercenary.[5] While he does engage in occasional protective acts, the Man With No Name is aware that such deeds are random and of little consequence. True heroism must elude him. In the traditional western, it is the heros' function to clear the land of evil so that civilization—women, children, schools, banks, stores, and churches—can safely expand into the frontier. No Daniel Boone, the Man With No Name cannot make the land safe for domesticity. Speaking to Silvanito, a kind of Sancho-Panza sidekick who befriends him, the Man With No Name states, "'The Baxters are over there. The Rojos there. Me, I'm right in the middle.'" In fact, the very land the Man With No Name inhabits is remarkably undomesticated. The stage-set town lacks the usual amenities; there are few women, and the desert is devoid of cattle, water, and any other elements that might allow "civilization" to prosper.

As a middleman, the Man With No Name understands that his survival is dependent upon his ability to read signs, to obtain information, and to confuse the more powerful personalities who surround him. "In these parts, a man's life often depends upon a mere scrap of information," instructs one of the villains. This line becomes a repetitive refrain in the course of the film. In keeping with this notion, the Man With No Name engages in a variety of espionage activities, climbing on ledges, jumping through windows, and worming through crawlspaces in order to obtain desirable "information." Self-consciously spoofing the film's genre, Silvanito observes that "it's like playing cowboys and Indians." In an era haunted by the question of espionage, and the cost of not having the "right" information, the Man With No Name acts out this cultural concern, representing the American Everyman's desire to know and simultaneously mocking and thereby disempowering the cold war spy game.

The very conflict, which defines the nonexistent town of San Miguel, references the American political climate. Ruled by two rival factions—the Rojos (the Reds) and the Anglo Baxters—the community is riddled by the deaths caused in the wake of their conflict. By the film's conclusion, only the unarmed, unseen figures locked inside behind closed doors—the bell-ringer, the saloonkeeper, the undertaker, and the Man With No Name—remain alive, and the town is largely depopulated. The immediate suggestion is that the accepted violence of the west must ultimately lead to a fearsome apocalypse, and clearly this sentiment had resonance with a populace engaging in practice air raid drills. But as Reed and Thompson note in their study of Baudrillard, Deleuze, and the western, this violence also becomes a kind of semiotic choreography, a code that represents a critique and disembodiment of the "real" as much as the "real" itself. Thus, the exaggerated violence becomes an exposure of the conventional western topos, and a metanarrative on the genre itself.[6]

The Rojos, with their Latino heritage, their laughable pseudo-masculinity, their unshaven faces, and army fatigue-style clothing, make obvious reference to the "Reds" in Cuba and Latin America. They provide parodic portrayals of the images of Fidel Castro and Che Guevara upon which the public had fixated. More significantly, the personages of the Rojos successfully conflate the image of the distant, threatening Other with the figure of the Mexican border bandit.[7] The Baxters, who possess an obviously Anglo name that is commonplace in the western, and wear Levi's and bandannas, are the Rojo's chief rivals. John Baxter is the town sheriff and thus the Baxters' power bears the mantle of legitimacy. But the horrors to which the village has been subjected—the constant killings, bombings, ongoing bilateral deception, and the film's final fiery holocaust—make any concept of legitimacy problematic.

The Rojos and the Baxters are engaged in a power game of perpetual killing that has transformed San Miguel into "the deadest town I've ever seen." As the Man With No Name enters the town, he is cautioned by the bell-ringer that the bell may very well soon toll for him. Explains the saloonkeeper, "here you can gain respect only by killing other people." This critique of racially inspired violence flies in the face of the more established western, which was often defined by the race divisions between Indians and settlers. Hallmark westerns, like John Ford's *The Searchers* (1956), were based upon the savagery of the nonwhite Other. Ethan (John Wayne) is forced to rescue the violated and abducted little Debbie (Natalie Wood) in order to establish familial order. Her rescue is followed by a massacre that is paralleled by Leone's destruction of San Miguel. In this sense, as the pale skinned are rescued from the darker Other, the earlier conventions explored racial anxieties, and suggested that the resulting violence was necessary. [8] When the Man With No Name rescues Marisal, no order results. It is thus an act of caprice with no moral claim. Moreover, she is a Latina; the woman represented in the film's captivity narrative is the Other.

A Fistful of Dollars suggests that the moral corruption of the dark Rojos extends also to the paler Baxters. Even while entertaining viewers with its comic depictions of Latinos, the film mocks notions of racial superiority.[9] While the film's chief villain is evidently Latino, nearly all of the characters are involved in villainy. There is no moral high ground.

The film's central drama concerns a series of captivities that can reach no satisfactory conclusion. Marisal, whose very name establishes her as a fallen virgin, is desired and eventually stolen away by the scheming Ramón Rojo. He keeps her locked up for his own use, away from her husband and her baby, aptly named Jesus. The Man With No Name is touched, although as he himself comments, he is not sure why. "You remind me of someone I used to know," he tells her but viewers cannot know if this someone was another woman or the man himself in some earlier more idealistic incarnation. Marisal is rescued, but the town of San Miguel can never be safe for her. The Man With No Name sends her down the road with her husband, holding her baby, and riding a donkey as she moves into exile in order to save her child. She is Mary, rushing into Egypt with the infant messiah, except that Marisal has experienced no annunciation and has no "promised land" in sight. Jesus has no destiny and thus no agenda. If he is a messiah, he is a savior without a promise and without hope.

As in the conventional western, the Man With No Name is forced to fight. He is captured and tortured in scenes far more graphic than those that composed earlier films. While John Wayne is occasionally wounded, Alan Ladd as Shane endures a few punches, and the Virginian acquires a seemingly bloodless wound, the Man With No Name suffers real abuse. In images that parallel the treatments of POWs during the Korean War and the suspected torments of Gary Powers, the man is tormented and interrogated. A reclining Ramón Rojo laughs while his henchmen grind the bones

in Eastwood's hand, tear his face, and bloody his torso. Their apparent purpose—like the feared interrogators of the cold war—is information; they
want to know where Marisal is hidden.

The Man With No Name must, of necessity, endure and escape, dem-
onstrating and parodying the perennially resourceful nature of Americans.
Despite the brutality of his punishment he lives, seeking refuge first in a
coffin and then in a self-constructed underground bunker that can only
represent a fallout shelter. As the Rojos search for him, the Baxters' com-
pound and the entire town of San Miguel are destroyed by fire bombs. As
Leone's camera pans the village, the water towers take on the eerie appearance of missile silos.

Eastwood's body, as the Man With No Name, takes on a significance
that eclipses the bodies of western heroes before him. His torso and limbs
are bared, his posture and expression eroticized. He offers new aesthetic
conception of the western hero. Paul Smith, in his essay "Eastwood
Bound," maintains that the erotic and even masochistic appearance that
became associated with Eastwood represents a complicating development
in the body of the western. The masculine frontier hero is never really able
to resolve the narrative contradictions that confront the western, argues
Smith. The frontiersman is always the man who must establish order
through violence, and is further a man who so much loves the pristine
frontier that he must develop and destroy it. Eastwood's body, concludes
Smith, exalts in these contradictions, indulging in pain that expresses the
conflict that must destroy him. But along with representing narrative dis-
junction, the tortured body of Eastwood indicates how far removed
Leone's work has become from conventional cinema.

As the viewer contemplates the distorted form of Eastwood, argues
Smith, the cultural contradictions implicit in the figure of the frontiersman
are forgotten. In the place of this contradictory representation is what
might be termed "hysterical residue" (Berger, Wallis, Watson 82). This
"residue" is the bodily record of unresolved and unrepresentable conflict,
which finally forces the masculine body of Eastwood to revert to a state of
objectification, effectively feminizing and fetishizing it.

So violent is Leone's work that the torn body of Eastwood becomes the
essence of the cultural production. His pain becomes unimportant and finally gratuitous, for the reality of the body in pain supersedes any intellectual content. The objectified body becomes "feminine," and this tropic
shift is accentuated by the fact that instead of reveling in the pleasure traditionally associated with the baring of the male body, Eastwood revels in
pain. Smith reveals that, "in the cultural production of this phallocentric

society, masculinity is represented first of all as a particular nexus of pleasure . . . Within such a representation something escapes or is left unmanaged. The hysterical is always what exceeds the phallic" (Berger, Wallis, Watson, 94–95). Eastwood, or the Man With No Name, then offers a role reversal to the viewer. In his exaggerated masculinity and overexposed body, The Man With No Name mimics rather than mirrors masculinity, and the end effect is a dissolution of patriarchal discourse. He is at once both the emblematic man of the postwar epoch and the man unmade/unmanned by that same era. The western, that untrammeled terrain of the phallus, has become feminine.

The unraveling masculinity of the Man With No Name is highly significant because this deconstruction must impact the larger culture. Patriarchy and masculinity are merely aspects of the larger society. Decentering masculine identity becomes a vehicle for reexamining culture as a whole. And indeed, Leone's film does this. As its countless phallic architectural spaces become fiery and then collapse, the fusion between violence and masculinity becomes evident. The final preserved space becomes one of destruction and decay. The apocalyptic (rather than heroic) nature of the phallus is revealed. It is an agent of destruction rather than salvation. Coupled with this critique is Leone's insistent irony, once again. The phallus is reduced to the tool of slapstick and, with this gesture, threatens a phallus-centered discourse.

As the underground Man With No Name nurses himself and reforges his identity, he sends out his two friends to discover covert information. Unlike his more romantic predecessors in the cinematic terrain, the Man With No Name understands that it is information—secret, arcane, political knowledge—that must triumph. This information proves to be even more valid than the phallus. Learning that Ramón Rojo always shoots for the heart, the Man With No name creates a bulletproof vest. He places this under his serape and goes out to exploit the weakness of his enemy. "You will lose," Ramón tells him, for "[w]hen a man with a Winchester meets a man with a .45, the man with the .45 will die." Ramón then indulges in a brief orgy of fondling his enormous gun. But the Man With No Name uses his own special, rebuilt .45, a military weapon that was used by the army in Vietnam. Thus, he blows Ramón Rojo away, aided more by information than by his well-armed masculinity.

Of course, the town of San Miguel is not saved by the removal of the Baxters and the Rojos. In the post–World War II era there are no more overwhelming victories. Annihilation is, at best, simply delayed another day or two. The Man With No Name follows Marisal's road out of town remarking "'Me? Here in the middle? Too dangerous.'" Unlike his heroic predecessors, the Man With No Name does not leave a valley now ready for domestic tranquility; he simply leaves while he's still ahead. As it offers a portrait of decomposing masculinity in a decomposed town, Leone's vision presents a portrait of the postmodern man.

For a Few Dollars More

Knowledge, writes Lyotard in *The Postmodern Condition*, is the ultimate postmodern commodity. Instead of seeking gold fields or even new lands, the successful contemporary person seeks knowledge—a knowledge that has a pragmatic applicability. This knowledge, however imperfect, can be marketed, and the market will no longer be limited to a few "players" or companies. The commodity market for useful data is worldwide; and thus, alliances to particular groups or even nations is made obsolete. Writes Lyotard: "Knowledge in the form of an informational commodity indispensable to productive power is already and will continue to be a major—perhaps the major—stake in the worldwide competition for power. . . . [N]ation-states will one day fight for control of information, just as they battled in the past for control of territory and afterwards for control of access to and exploitation of raw materials and cheap labor" (5). Command of information distinguishes the new "world order," and in the struggle for command a new form of mercenary will be created. Continues Lyotard, "data banks are the Encyclopedia of tomorrow. They transcend the capacity of their users. They are 'nature' for the modern man" (51).

This new "nature" is explored by Sergio Leone. Released in 1965, *For a Few Dollars More* provides a commentary on the commodification of knowledge, and also critiques the "informatics" of the cold war. While earlier westerns had heroically detailed how territory and "justice" were won, Leone is concerned with the process of acquiring information. *For a Few Dollars More* thus does not really concern itself with establishing a frontier order (like *The Virginian*), or a rescue (as in *The Searchers*), or with the development of masculinity (*Red River*). Instead, it concerns the monetary value—and "paralogy" if you will—of knowing.

The film's protagonists, Colonel Mortimer and Manko (Eastwood), differ dramatically from traditional frontier heroes. Like the mercenary, they have no national or communal allegiance. Instead, they sell themselves and their highly commodified knowledge to the highest bidder. Moreover, the nature of their knowledge is vastly different from that claimed by other frontier heroes. Previous cinematic heroes followed the model of Natty Bumppo, and achieved their ends through their specialized knowledge of "nature"—a nature that included the savage Other, of course. But Mortimer and Manko are distanced from nature. Theirs is instead a knowledge of technology and things—guns, watches, explosives, and, most particularly, methods of surveillance. They exist outside the "natural" world, and like Lyotard's "modern man," the nature they command is that of the data bank. This is highly significant, for this shift allows Leone to remove his film from the celebrated natural environment that is the traditional set of the frontier story. Instead, Leone enacts his drama within a transient, surreal landscape that receives little attention. The small details are more important than the larger territory. The foxhole displaces the wider expanding territory.

Set against the escalating war in Vietnam and increasing anxiety about the worldwide role of the Central Intelligence Agency, *For a Few Dollars More* interrogates the quality of life in the foxhole, focusing upon finite issues rather than on national narrative. In Sergio Leone's disjunctive landscapes, narrative truths seem irrelevant. This viewpoint was not limited to Leone's work, for a general distrust of monotheistic narrative was beginning to mark the culture. "God is dead," proclaimed a cover of *Time* magazine in 1965. The magazine issue then proceeded to examine the new cultural and political ethos. Leone's film makes a similar pronouncement.

For a Few Dollars More opens with an overbright, long-distance image of a lone rider crossing a technicolor Eden. He is alone, and the too abundant landscape is revealed to be the wilderness paradise that is a familiar trope in the western. (Indeed, the landscape is really too lush to provide a "realistic" depiction of the American frontier. Its green foliage has more in common with the jungles and deltas that will soon become familiar elements in the emerging genre of the Vietnam film.) The figure of the rider suddenly collapses, struck by gunfire from a hidden opponent. This disturbing scene then dissolves into the film's credits, and a troubling epigraph appears on the screen. "Where life had no value, death sometimes had its price. That is why the bounty hunters appeared." Screening a scant twenty months after the John F. Kennedy assassination, the disrupted Edenic scene evokes the quality of a disrupted Camelot.

The opening scene of the film has little relation to the plot, which finally concerns the problematic relationships between the elderly Colonel Mortimer, Manko, and the bandit, El Indio.[10] Theirs is a story of espionage and counter-espionage. The real dilemma of the film hinges on a series of twisting, internecine alliances that are formed, broken, and reformed, re-configuring the shifting power structure of the movie. All three of the main characters cheat and spy on one another. Even Manko and Mortimer, who are reportedly partners, lie, recite incomplete truths, and continuously attempt to subvert one another.

El Indio shares these same qualities, but he also displays them with less finesse, which is perhaps his most damning quality. He is a parody of the Latino thought to be lurking just south of the American border. Swarthy and Latin in appearance, his clothing is dirty, his laughter hysterical, and his violence often inexplicable. When he escapes from prison early in the film, his first act is to kill his cell mate, an individual who is in fact responsible for making the escape possible. "Adios, Amigo," laughs El Indio, in an ironic aside that becomes a continuous refrain in the film. As the story progresses, we learn that El Indio has an enormous price on his head, and that Manko and Mortimer are both pursuing him (often secretly and individually) for the reward.

Mortimer's reasons for the pursuit are also represented to be personal, and at first the viewer is tempted to "read" the film as a more traditional revenge tale. Years before the viewer is informed, El Indio raped and killed Mortimer's young wife, wounded Mortimer, and then took an antique watch that had been given to Mortimer by his bride. El Indio uses the watch to time his diabolical executions, and each vision of the object seems to propel Mortimer into a nostalgic flashback. The watch acquires a nearly fetishized nature, for the very presence of the object reminds Mortimer of the romance that has been erased from the world. As he contemplates his loss and the watch, he is very nearly a modernist Fisher King, recalling his great wound. "Tell me Colonel," queries Manko, "were you ever young?" The very question implies that Manko still retains some youthful idealism and wishes to reawaken this sentiment in Mortimer. This image is perpetuated when the narrator informs the viewer that Mortimer was once the most brave, effective, and honored soldier in the Civil War. "But now he's reduced to being a bounty hunter," mourns the storyteller. It is easy thus to view Mortimer as a man who has lost Eden. However, Leone problematizes this narrative.

Leone's film allows for no lost Eden and unsettles any notions regarding a vanished Camelot. In the course of the film, we learn that Manko and Mortimer are competing for the reward, and that, in fact, Mortimer's golden age of innocence never really existed. In an unlikely and nearly comic plot shift, the viewer learns that there were two identical watches, and that Mortimer's wife gave two gifts. She was at once Mortimer's wife and El Indio's sister and lover; she betrayed them both by committing suicide while in El Indio's embrace. There is no Eden, Leone seems to say, there is only faulty information. In fact, Mortimer's marriage, its dissolution, and his long pursuit of El Indio are all the result of incomplete knowledge and a vague, misplaced nostalgia.

Once again, the essential power of knowledge is stressed throughout the film. El Indio makes a habit of killing those who "know too much." Manko makes it a practice to communicate false knowledge. At one point, he joins El Indio's band in order to convince them of false information. Manko also sends fraudulent information over the telegraph wires, and, several frames later, cuts the wires themselves, proclaiming tacitly that control over the technologies of information creates power.

The use and concealment of power are further revealed in the continual bluffing engaged in by each character. For amusement, Manko and Mortimer shoot at one another, coming as close to killing one another as they possibly can, and acting as if each commands some specialized knowledge that will save them from harm. Even the small children who watch recognize the game of "chicken": their games are "just like that games that we play" remark the boys. Leone mocks the tropic gunfight of the west, recognizing it, as do the children, as ignoble and more about skill and information than about honor. But as he mocks the trope through repetition, Leone also undermines the genre itself and questions the notion of conceptual categories.

In this same vein, the film satirizes the moral claims traditionally made by the western. Both Manko and Mortimer are bounty hunters, unethical and self-serving. Mortimer always wears black, rides a black horse, stops trains, and interrupts naked women in their boudoirs. Manko wears the dirty serape which was Eastwood's signature in this cinematic trilogy. He too takes what is convenient—women, hotel rooms, and money. Their claim to moral authority is based on style (they look better than anyone else), and on information. "I have my sources," each character repeats to the other.

As the film closes, Manko is portrayed as the "natural" man of the late twentieth century. The beautiful world to which Mortimer has constantly alluded has never existed. As Manko takes on the role of Mortimer's son, he realizes that his inheritance is troubled. He has been given a false nostalgia. The film's final scenes take place in a nearly deserted fort, which again is highly reminiscent of the forts displayed in Vietnam films. The fort is under attack, and as the strange black and purple light falls on Manko's face, the light takes on the appearance of camouflage paint.

Approaching in the dappled light, the attackers practice the stealth and covert moves of guerilla fighters. The viewer does not know who owns the fort in the abandoned city of Agua Caliente. Neither identity nor moral position is evident. Manko is preparing to engage is some unknown act of espionage. As the film details the failure of nostalgia and idealism, it celebrates, finally, only "knowing." Its cinematic iconography moves relentlessly toward the political "hot water" (the town, Agua Caliente) and terrain of Vietnam. Vietnam is the cost, the text implies, that will be exacted as the price of false nostalgia.

The Good, the Bad and the Ugly

In his critical work, *Postmodernist Fiction*, Brian McHale comments on the ways in which postmodern fiction establishes what he calls an "ontological universe," a space that incorporates "jostling worldviews," a "complex jigsaw puzzle of 'subuniverses of meaning'" into a conceptual machinery that allows for representation of the marginal (37). More simply put, postmodern or contemporary discourse allows for the representation of the repressed or marginal within the conventional tropes of the literary. Postmodernism, continues McHale, has a "repertoire of strategies . . . in order to foreground the ontological structure of text and world." These strategies include the incorporation of a "flickering" effect, disturbing the continuum between the text and the world. This process is further developed by the "spatial displacement of words and by the disruption of "real-world" history. From this disrupted history the text creates a new history, what McHale terms a disruptive "apocryphal" history.[11]

In particular, McHale notes how the process of parody operated within cold war culture. The cold war with its demonizing of the "evil empire" created a hermeneutic that divided discourse and semiotics into a binary, manichean form. Parody allows for the "bleeding" of category and genre into a more pluralistic conversation, thereby breaking down the exclusionary aspects of cold war conservatism, and the creation of an unlicensed history (44).

Years before tracts on postmodernism would appear, Sergio Leone offered his viewers a glimpse at the new ontological landscape, a disruptive and unreal landscape that in its apparent lack of "reality" would closely mimic and simultaneously critique the existing world. Leone presents his audience with disjunctive and preposterous scenes, with chaotic and undefined spaces, and with parody that would remake accepted cultural conventions. Using the genre of the western, Leone uses cinematic parody to redefine the landscape and history of the frontier. Perhaps his most famous film, *The Good, the Bad and the Ugly* (1966), completes his western Eastwood trilogy. As a text, the film is openly self-parodic, and is utterly dislocated from its generic terrain.

The dislocated landscape is apparent from the film's opening scene. The film begins with a strangely silent and violent fourteen-minute sequence of footage that can only be understood through the confused ethos of Vietnam. The film text displays a small town, its location and inhabitants unknown. Men sneak up, firing through the window of the bar. There is an explosion, but the results are unclear. It is impossible to know exactly who is alive and who is wounded. The explosion is an inexplicable act of terrorism.

Then, the scene shifts; the viewer's attention is focused on a piece of unidentified desert. A lone man is being attacked by three other men. Suddenly, Eastwood appears. The three men are shot, and Eastwood joins the other man, casually smoking his trademark cigar. For a moment, the viewer is allowed to assume that this time Eastwood will perform a heroic role. But the scene shifts again. Eastwood appears again with the man from the desert who is now a prisoner, trussed and tossed on the sheriff's steps. Finally, well into the film, the audience realizes that Eastwood—once again the Man With No Name—is a bounty hunter. The audience relaxes; perhaps all will be explained.

But another shift occurs. The prisoner swears and spits. The next frame depicts a gallows scene. A shot sounds, the rope is pulled taut, the audience tenses and expects to find the condemned man dead. Instead, he is free; the Man With No Name has broken the rope with a fabled single shot, and he rides away carrying the escaped prisoner. It is only at this point that the film breaks into dialogue, thereby informing the viewer that a "sting" has just been witnessed. The rescue was prearranged, and the bounty hunter has turned con man. The next day he will move onto the next town and repeat the performance. Every trope or image—the single gunshot, the public hanging, the sheriff, the prisoner, and the violence—is parodied. Although there is no defined location, the viewer implicitly understands that this is a disrupted landscape.

Periodically, during these early frames, the camera freezes, and across the film a comic-book style caption occurs. In hot-pink letters, characters are designated as "good," "bad," or "ugly," with the implication that unless these arbitrary distinctions were made by the director, such classifications would be impossible. There are no givens or absolutes in this landscape; everything is playful naming. This ambiguity is further demonstrated by the moral collapse of nearly all of the characters. The Man With No Name has degenerated into a man who exploits and betrays all alliances, motivated solely by money. Mortimer has evolved into an evil Union sergeant, and this decay is mirrored by every military or authority figure. There is some discussion of the Civil War, which emerges, like the Vietnam conflict, as a senseless, inexplicable struggle, conducted in a jungle-like environment wherein the Union soldiers cannot be discerned from the Confederate players. Neither character appears to have any real memory of an earlier life.

The cartoon-like commentary that begins the film serves to inform the viewer that this is not a "serious" western. The result of the hot-pink cinematic marginalia is that Eastwood has more in common with the television "Batman" of the same era than with John Wayne. In this film, everything is a game and there is little attempt at realism. Distances are collapsed; people walk ninety miles in a matter of an hour or two. Marcia Landy has commented on these landscapes, suggesting that they are at once consistent with the metaphorical stylistics of Italian theater, opera, and cinema, and that they construct a metaphorical space in which Leone can stage his comic parodies of genre (Landy 49–51). Jane Tompkins, in *West of Everything*, connects the hero's body to the land, contending that his social relationships, spirituality, and destiny are located in the dusty topos geography (82).

In this space where nothing seems to be remembered, an apocryphal history unfolds; a remade, dubious, and perhaps illegitimate history of both the nineteenth century and the history of the 1960s. Lest the viewer miss the reference to the moral morass that defines the film, Leone provides numerous allusions to Vietnam. The soldiers are equipped with semiautomatic weapons; catastrophic bombs explode; and "Half Soldier," an amputee, sits on the town steps and collects spare change. Long scenes take place in POW camps, and the men walk—"hump"—miles of unmarked difficult terrain. The dislocation that is evident in the film makes it impossible even to discern in what direction the west lies. The topography shifts, and Leone draws a new conceptual map of the era.

The Good, the Bad and the Ugly, far from being escapist fiction, acknowledges both the existence of the Vietnam war, cold war hostilities, and the ambiguity of their moral terrain. Further, Leone suggests that the simple binarisms that characterized both conventional westerns and cold war culture in general can no longer apply. Even the film's title—raising as it does a trio of categories—collapses oppositions. It is possible, the text of the film argues, that there is only the messy, the difficult, the complicated, and the apocryphal. In a semicomic scene, a minor character informs the Man With No Name, as he indulges in surveillance, that "there are two kinds of spurs, my friend. Those that come in by the door [meaning conventional spurs] and those that come in by the window." The comment is characteristically absurd, however, for the Man With No Name learns that the spurs are the same. It is the situation—who is wearing them and in what context—that shifts. There are many kinds of spurs, and the variety is defined by the objects that reference the spur rather than by any essential distinction. To overread the spur, to suggest that there is some essential goodness or badness to be defined by its topos, is to miss the point and thus risk death.

As the screen detonates with automatic weapon fire and high-power explosions, the viewer's very sense of time and space is collapsed. Clearly, the designated time period—the post–Civil War, reconstruction era—is only meant to confuse the viewer. The action takes place instead within some contemporary or even future terrain. There is no temporal correspondence; the viewer cannot tell whether hours, days, or even months have passed. In the same way, the scene moves relentlessly from a desert, to some eastern postwar village, and finally to some indistinguishable verdant and exotic location. Conventional codes cannot be read; like the spurs they lead only to absurd abstraction.

As in all of Leone's works, *The Good, the Bad and the Ugly* demystifies the western hero and his colonial quest. As Richard Slotkin argues in his *Regeneration Through Violence*, the fundamental goal of the frontiersman and his cinematic counterpart has been the extension of "civilization."[12] Such a goal assumes that there is something that resembles the lofty notion of civilized society, and further that it can be defined by projecting it over its binary opposite—the savage Other. David Davis makes a similar point in his essay on westerns, "The Hero and the Frontier." Davis argues: "[T]he cowboy myth . . . is probably a more influential social force than the actual cowboy ever was. . . . [T]he descent is a direct evolution from the Western scout to Cooper. . . . [T]he ideal cowboy fights for justice, risks his life to make the dismal little cowtowns safe for law-abiding, respectable citizens" (Davis 27). For Davis, the frontiersman's milieu is thus finally utopian. In his exhaustive study of the genre of the western, Will Wright makes a similar comment on the structure of the hero, arguing that the encoded mythology that shapes the western requires this heroic presence.

Leone dismantles nostalgia and narrative idealism. For not only are Leone's heroes remarkably unheroic, but there is no utopian world to be saved. The world Leone opts to mirror is the world created out of the binary western fantasies about good and evil, heroism and villainy. It is a world of horrifying and absurd violence, a haze of smoke through which one can only emerge through good luck and arcane bits of knowledge. It is a world in which violence is coded and becomes the only possible lexicon, and it is a world of metalanguage, wherein all discourse can only serve as meditation upon itself. *The Good, the Bad and the Ugly* suggests that, rather than defending utopia, the western hero is only successful in contributing to the creation of a violent dystopia and to the creation of a self-contained language. Remarking upon the development of the post-Leone western, the self-referential language and semiotics of westerns, and the direction of his own career after the multivalent role of the Man With No Name, Eastwood commented, "I do all the stuff that John Wayne would never do" (Frayling 154). Leone's films, Eastwood implicitly understood, violate generic lexicon.[13]

Speaking of "cowboys and sundogs," Brian McHale argues that postmodern fiction poses the questions of "how is knowledge transmitted . . . ? . . . How is a world constituted? Are there alternative worlds, and if so, how are they constituted?" (*Constructing Postmodernism* 247). McHale argues that these questions are interpolated and explored frequently through the depiction of space and virtual space. Postmodern texts, according to McHale, often depend on the creation of space and require, within this space, the construction of other communities. This spatial component is inherited from the medieval romance and lends itself to the postmodern textual quest. Continues McHale:

In medieval romance, the category of world normally the unrepresentable absolute horizon of all experience and perception, is itself made an object of representation through a particular metaphorical use of enclosed spaces within the romance world: castles, enchanted forests, walled gardens, bowers, etc. Such symbolic enclosures, functioning as scale-models or miniature analogues of the world, bring into view the normally invisible horizons of world. . . . Space, in other words, becomes . . . [in medieval romance and postmodern fiction] an all-purpose tool of "doing" ontology—a means of exploring ontology in fiction as well . . . as the ontology of fiction. (247)[14]

The representation, as well as, the distortion and dislocation of space, becomes a way of showing shifts in what Jameson has called the "conceptual map." These ruptures become ontological codes. Leone's dystopic, disassociated spaces work in precisely this fashion.

No Horizons

Much has been written about the cinematic western, with some critics contending that the genre reified the racialized violence that characterized the colonial mission into the frontier. Other writers maintain that the sophisticated western provided a critique of violence. Writing about John Ford's *The Searchers*, in his exhaustive critical study *Gunfighter Nation*, Richard Slotkin talks about the mixed reception of the film, suggesting: "The moral confusion of the ending is responsible for two recurrent misreadings of the film. A "left" misreading sees it as an exemplar of the very racism it decries. A "right" misreading sees Ethan Edwards [the misanthropic racist rescuer of "Little Debbie"] as an entirely heroic figure whose harsh manner and personal isolation are the consequence of his devotion to mission and his unique understanding of the red [savage] menace" (471–72).

But Leone takes neither conventional path through the genre of the western, indeed, he is not concerned with finding moral readings. In this way, he escapes what Landy has termed the "binarism" of the typical western, as well as the more simple and binary arguments about the nature of both the western and postmodernism itself. Instead, Leone offers a view of an entirely different moral space, where issues of accuracy and misinterpretation can make no sense. There is no meaning to the landscape—and that is in fact its meaning—and there is no one way to read the film. There are only codes, tropes, and images that have become detached from any stable signifier.

Leone's apocryphal history has displaced the conventional west of *The Searchers* and replaced it with a metaphorical nonplace. For him the west becomes:

A place of confrontation, but not as a closed field offering the spectacle of a struggle among equals . . . rather it is a "non-place," a pure distance, which indicates that the adversaries do belong to a common space. . . . In a sense only a single drama is ever staged in this non-place, the needlessly repeated play of dominations. . . . It is fixed throughout history in rituals, in meticulous procedures. . . . It establishes marks of its power . . . by no means to temper violence but to satisfy it . . . [it] permits the perpetual instigations of new dominations and the staging of meticulously repeated scenes of violence. (Foucualt 84, 85)

For Leone, the very agenda of colonialism is a problem that must always erase the notion of utopia. The horrors of the cold war and Vietnam removed in fact the possibility of happy endings and, in fact, maintained that there never was such a possibility. Sergio Leone credits the film *Shane* as one of his inspirations, but his own work confounds the very structure of *Shane* (Frayling 157). It is no longer possible, suggests Leone, for Alan Ladd, as Shane, to ride off happily into the sunset. Further, Leone implies that this very idyllic act itself was complicitous in the disaster of the cold war. The Man With No Name realizes this paradigm. Even as he repeats that all he wants is sufficient money "to buy a little place" of his own and "settle down," the Man With No Name realizes that utopia is an illusion that he can only exploit and that there is no pastoral life. Leone's films use conventional western semiotic code to mark the eternal absence of utopic possibility.

New Horizons

The great director of western films, John Ford, possessed a unique cinematic signature. Many of his films closed with a representation of a lone rider moving into a vast horizon and sunset. In these scenes, the hero is eclipsed, absorbed into the larger "errand into the wilderness" that surrounds him. His vision is obvious, his heroism unencumbered. Sergio Leone opts to forgo these enlarged views, instead encompassing his anti-hero within a restricted and disassociated space. In the wake of the failing new frontier, even knowing which way is west proves to be problematic. There are no luminous horizons, and thus the Man With No Name cannot find a way out.

Similarly, the Man With No Name has no central occupation. Ford's re-imagined west is closed off by looming buildings, undesignated mountain ranges, and by Leone's technique of focusing upon close-ups rather than utilizing longshots. Accordingly, when the Man With No Name departs, the viewer can never predict in what direction he will move.

Further, Leone's technique suggests something more. His films tell local stories; the relationships between the protagonists' experiences and the larger social narrative is never clarified. Directors like John Ford, John Sturges, and George Stevens were able to place their narratives within the context of some national legend. But for Leone and his era, all narratives are absorbed, caught up in some local plurality. No single horizon is possible. There is only information and the individual mimetic acts and parodies that have lost the source of their inspiration. This condition, in fact, constitutes the postmodern condition, Lyotard reminds us in *Just Gaming*. The collapse of a single narrative horizon allows instead for a horizon of justice.

"[It's] a total blank," says the Eastwood protagonist in *High Plains Drifter* (1973), parodying the phrasing and atmospherics of the earlier spaghetti westerns. He comments, as well, on the misty blank that formulates postmodernism. Is this the blank of existential, late modernist despair, or is it the space of jubilant, liberating play? Neither suggests Leone's texts. It is just space, blank space, against which we as viewers must write our own apocryphal histories. It is a terrain outside the binarism of critical debate, a space that shifts, cannot be defined, and thus always demands fresh cartography.

Notes

1. See Peter Bondanella's *Italian Cinema: From Neorealism to the Present*. Bloomington: Indiana University Press, 1993, and also Marcia Landy's "Which Way is West," *Boundary 2*, spring, 1996.

2. For further discussion of this point, see both Fredric Jameson's *Postmodernism Or The Cultural Logic of Late Capitalism*, Durham: Duke University Press, 1991, and Brian McHale's *Constructing Postmodernism*, especially pages 145–80.

3. *New York Times*, like all national newspapers, covered this event extensively. See in particular, "U-2 Shooting," *New York Times*, 5-9-60, p. 1+.

4. As in the case of the Powers incident, these events were widely reported in "serious" journals, tabloids, and even in elementary school *Weekly Readers*. This particular reference is taken from "Soviets in Cuba," *New York Times*, 10-13-62, p. 1+.

5. Since Leone's trilogy, the bounty-hunter as hero (or antihero) has become a stock character of the revived western. Indeed, Eastwood recouped this character when he played the bounty-hunter, Munny, in the film *The Unforgiven* (1993).

6. In this sense, Leone's work closely parallels the much more recent cinematic efforts of Quentin Tarrantino and his *Pulp Fiction* (1995).

7. The figure of the Mexican is often conflated with the image of the Indian in American culture, to form a single idea of an alien dark Other. The fear is further exacerbated when the Mexican is defined as a "half-breed," or is found guilty of comingling his/her flesh with an Anglo lover. Both Richard Slotkin in *Gunfighter Nation* and Jane Tompkins in *West of Everything* point out that the rescued victims of Indian captivities—actual or fictional—were largely shunned because of the implicit belief that penetration by the Other had alienated and "Otherized" the retrieved captives. In *The Searchers*, Ethan Edwards has to be restrained from killing "Little Debbie," the object of his seven-year search, after he realizes that she has wed and slept with Scar. Debbie has become, for Ethan Edwards, a half-breed.

8. It is interesting to note that Jane Tompkins makes the argument in her *Sensational Designs* that tales using the captivity narrative were immensely popular during the nineteenth century. Tompkins regards this popularity as a measure of the nation's racial anxiety. It may be that the westerns from 1940 to 1965 mirrored these same racialized concerns.

9. As Landry comments, the use of this type of comedy was commonplace in

Italian film. She refers to this stylistic topos as *comedia dell'arte* and suggests that it is nearly always, in some way, disruptive of hegemony.

10. The name "El Indio" suggests an ironic commentary on American concerns about the Other, and is an example of how Native Americans and Mexicans are conflated to form a single image of the Other.

11. See McHale, pages 86–90, and pages 179–202.

12. Most of Richard Slotkin's work deals in some way with this single mythology: the hunter/trailblazer's unceasing domestication of the frontier territory. Slotkin pays particular, overt attention to this when discussing the Daniel Boone legends. Boone, at least for Slotkin, is the primary type upon which later legends and heroes were fashioned.

13. Paying tribute to the master of the new language of the western, Eastwood acknowledged Leone in his dedication to the *Unforgiven*, a film Eastwood regarded as an "antiwestern."

14. For a further discussion of landscape in the western, see both Toby Reed and R. J. Thompson's essay "The Six-Gun Simulacrum: New Metaphors for an Old Genre."

Works Cited

Berger, Maurice, Brian Wallis, and Simon Watson, eds. *Constructing Masculinity*. New York: Routledge, 1995.

Bondanella, Peter. *Italian Cinema: From Neorealism to the Present*. Bloomington: Indiana University Press, 1993.

Davis, David. "The Hero and the Frontier." *The Western*, James Folsom, ed. Englewood Cliffs: Prentice-Hall, 1979.

Drinnon, Richard. *Facing West: The Metaphysics of Indian Hating and Empire Building*. Minneapolis: University of Minnesota Press, 1981.

Foucault, Michel. *Nietzsche, Genealogy and History*. New York: Pantheon Books, 1984.

Frayling, Christopher. *Spaghetti Westerns: Cowboys and Europeans from Karl May to Sergio Leone*. London: Routledge, 1981.

Landy, Marcia. "Which Way is America: Americanism and the Italian Western." *Boundary 2*. Vol. 23, No. 1, spring, 1996.

Lyotard, Jean-François. *The Postmodern Condition: A Report on Knowledge*. Minneapolis: University of Minnesota Press, 1984.

———. *Just Gaming*. Minneapolis: University of Minnesota Press, 1985.

McHale, Brian. *Postmodernist Fiction*. New York: Routledge, 1987.

———. *Constructing Postmodernism*. New York: Routledge, 1992.

McRobbie, Angela. *Postmodernism and Popular Culture*. New York: Routledge, 1994.

Reed, Toby, and R. J. Thompsom. "The Six-Gun Simulacrum: New Metaphors for an Old Genre." *Film Criticism*, spring, 1996.

Slotkin, Richard. *Regeneration Through Violence: The Mythology of the American Frontier*. Middletown, Ct.: Wesleyan University Press, 1973.

———. *Gunfighter Nation: The Mythology of the Frontier in Twentieth-Century America*. New York: HarperPerennial, 1992.

"Soviets in Cuba." *New York Times*, 10/13/62, 1.

Tompkins, Jane. *Sensational Designs: The Cultural Work of American Fiction*. New York: Oxford University Press, 1985.

————. *West of Everything: The Inner Life of Westerns*. New York: Oxford University Press, 1992.

"U-2 Shooting," *The New York Times*, 5/9/60, l.

Wright, Will. *Six Guns and Society: A Structural Study of the Western*. Berkeley: University of California Press, 1975.

Selected Filmography

A Fistful of Dollars. Sergio Leone. 1964.
For a Few Dollars More. Sergio Leone. 1965.
Fort Apache. John Ford. 1948.
Pulp Fiction. Quentin Tarrentino. 1995.
The Good, the Bad and the Ugly. Sergio Leone. 1966.
The Searchers. John Ford. 1956.
Shane. George Stevens. 1953.
The Unforgiven. Clint Eastwood. 1993.

CHAPTER SIX

Disruptive Genealogies: Louise Erdrich's *The Bingo Palace* and Native American Identities

> I want now to explore forms of cultural identity and political solidarity that emerge from the disjunctive temporalities of the national culture. This is a lesson of history to be learnt from those peoples whose histories of marginality have been most profoundly enmeshed in the antinomies of law and order—the colonized and women.
>
> —Homi Bhabha, *Dissemination*

> Once the bureaucrats sink their barbed pens into the lives of Indians, the paper starts flying, a blizzard of legal forms, a waste of ink by the gallon, a correspondence to which there is no end or reason. That's when I began to see what we were becoming, and the years have borne me out: a tribe of file cabinets and triplicates, a tribe of single-space documents, directives, policy. A tribe of pressed trees. A tribe of chicken-scratch that can be scattered by a wind, diminished to ashes by one struck match.
>
> —Louise Erdrich, *Tracks*

"Proof Positive in Indian Country"

In *The Bingo Palace* (1995), the fourth novel in her Turtle Mountain series, which also includes *Love Medicine* (1985), *Tracks* (1988), and *The Beet Queen* (1986), Louis Erdrich's young Chippewa Lipsha Morrissey eventually finds himself standing on a dusty reservation road, contemplating his vexing cultural identity.[1] There, amid the Turtle Mountain landscape allocated the Chippewa after their deterritorialization by the American government's reservation policies, Lipsha confronts a number of choices. On one side of the road passes Fleur Pillager, his reputed great-grandmother, mystic, witch, town-crank, and resider-over of secrets to his seemingly untraceable past. On the other side resides the reservation bureau and its promise of a band card, a kind of passport denoting his precise cultural and genealogical roots as a Chippewa.

At first Lipsha enters the government office. But once inside, he realizes the futility of his situation:

> I sit down again. I am waiting for proof-positive self-identification, a complicated thing in Indian Country. I am waiting for a band card, trying out of boredom to prove who I am—the useless son of a criminal father and mother who died with her hands full of snow—but in trying to prove myself to the authorities, I am having no luck, for Zelda is a solid force to reckon with. I don't have my enrollment and entitlement stabilized, not yet, nor do I have my future figured exactly out. Still, the reason I have been hanging out has just walked down the road. I stand there on the steps. Duplicates of applications and identification papers weigh down my hands. "Here." I shove them at Layla. She takes them. "File it under 'L' for Love Child," I say, walking off. (129)

Ultimately, Lipsha chooses to veer in Fleur Pilliger's direction. His dilemma and cultural position as a contemporary Native American trying to get "proof-positive" identification in Indian Country, however, underscores how Erdrich's texts actively engage the problematics of hybridity and postcolonial identity and its relation to Native American experience.

Erdrich herself has stated that the question of identity is primary in her fiction. As she puts it, her fiction is about the "mixed-blood" question of "Who am I from?"[2] Indeed, the problems associated with Native American identity are central to *The Bingo Palace* and other tetralogy texts. But while countless commentators have remarked on issues of identity and Erdrich's fiction, none have stressed how the texts—and *The Bingo Palace* in particular—actually unmask and critique a range of spectral relations that coalesce around the very idea of identity founded on notions of "blood." As Lipsha's plight suggests, "stability" and "proving" oneself to authorities involves reconciling his uncertain genealogical origins and past (a past intersected with nomadism and colonial interference) with federal agencies. For Lipsha, the question of his essentialized bloodlines leads directly to questions of legitimacy, "authenticity," and family.

It is through this inquiry, into the reflexive relationships between familial origins, legitimacy, property, and "blood," that Erdrich's Turtle Mountain novels critique the tyranny of colonial constructs and the way they affect those, like Lipsha, who live in what Iain Chambers has called the in-between spaces of a "broken world" (70). In *The Bingo Palace*, this critique unfolds against the polyvocal representations of the Chippewa and Turtle Mountain reservation past, and the present contestations among community members over land, status, and survivance. As Lipsha's plight illustrates, genealogy and "origins" prove central in these disputes, suggesting larger colonial relationships between heritage, origins, property, and identity.

Rather than articulating definitive lineage, Erdrich's presentation of vexed and troubled ancestral webs confound the reader, forcing us to reevaluate our conceptions concerning identity, family, and history. For Erdrich, genealogy emerges as trickster's game—a seductive pursuit seemingly offered to the reader but fraught with loopholes and contingencies, mimicry, fraudulent appearances, and playful, shifting signifiers—wherein "bloodlines" disrupt history and where some larger "genealogy" of spirit and sensibility resound and displace the familiar formulations of western heredity. Like the other Chippewas in Erdrich's novel, Lipsha finds himself on a journey requiring the negotiation of multiple cultural codes. For Lipsha, as for many contemporary Native Americans (and others who travel the in-between spaces of postcoloniality), identity amid this transcultural space involves an identification forged out of a complex hybridity, where resistance, tradition, and nomadic displacement converge. From this perspective, Erdrich's texts can be read as "enunciative," to use Homi Bhabha's phrase. As enunciative, they engage in what Bhabha has termed the "Third Space," compelling us to reconceive our notions concerning such constructs as identity, family, and community.

The "Third Space"

In the course of challenging such colonial inscriptions, Erdrich's work sketches a kind of multivoiced, twentieth-century history of South Dakota's Turtle Mountain Chippewa reservation. The reservation was established in 1882, after the Algonquian-speaking Chippewa had been driven West by encroaching settlers and Iroquois.[3] While the first novel, *Love Medicine*, establishes the contemporary problem of identity, historicizing it by providing the stories of the previous generation, *Tracks* moves backward in time to provide histories of the families that structure the other novels. *The Beet Queen* is largely occupied with the mostly-white town that exists near the boundaries of the reservation, and with the lives of some of its protagonists moving across the barrier into Native American life. But it is with *The Bingo Palace* that Erdrich's stories and histories find their culminating themes. In this last novel, Lipsha emerges as a sort of quixotic Native American everyman, overtly pondering the problems of identity, possession, and money. The son of the Leonard Peltier-like trickster-activist Gerry Nanapush and the wandering, lost June Kashpaw—who figure so prominently in *Love Medicine*—Lipsha is an innocent in a complex world.[4]

Speaking in simple, lyrical language, Lipsha tells of his predicament. Bright and sensitive, groomed finally for college, Lipsha leaves the reservation only to work in the nearby sugar factory. When he is eerily summoned by his grandmother Lulu, now the tribal chief, Lipsha returns to the reservation, knowing that he is bent on some particular errand, but unable to discern what it might be. He immediately encounters three people who force him to ponder who he is. Shawnee Ray, with whom he falls in love, forces him to explain his direction and to understand the patriarchal demands that have come to structure western concepts of love. Lyman Lamartine, relative and rival, employs him in his new gambling casino and introduces Lipsha to the necessity of money and the dilemma of commodification that faces today's Native American population. June, Lipsha's dead mother, reappears as an irate ghost, manipulating the luck inherent in *The Bingo Palace* and suggesting how arbitrary are our categories of understanding. Ultimately, Lipsha seeks to find a way to satisfactorily live his life beyond or outside the colonial categories that surround and haunt him.

Erdrich's framing of Lipsha's life as defined by issues of nomadism, colonial tyranny, personal questions of identity, and survivance indeed proves resonant with Homi Bhabha's explorations of "hybridity," and subaltern resistance. Displaced in a manner that is not dissimilar to the Chippewa experience, Bhabha gives voice to the subaltern predicament in which Lipsha finds himself. Bhabha ponders the problem of identity, suggesting that minority culture is so consumed by larger, hegemonic discourse that the vocabulary of resistance is frequently structured by mimicry and parody. Where then, he asks, is identity when any "authentic" self has been ravaged and displaced?

Minority discourse thus becomes for Bhabba a kind of hybridity itself, structured by a shifting instability between discursive worlds, constantly negotiated and renegotiated by what we know as postcolonial subjectivity. This very subjectivity allows the construction of an alternative discursive space, an "in-between" hybrid locality of representation, a "Third Space":

The bearers of hybrid identity . . . are caught in the discontinuous time of translation and negotiation . . . they are now free to negotiate and translate their cultural identities in a discontinuous intertextual temporality of cultural difference. The native intellectual who identifies the people with the "true national culture" will be disappointed. The people are now the very principle of "dialectical reorganization . . . [based] on the inscription and articulation of culture's hybridity. Top that and we would remember that it is the "inter"—the cutting edge of translation and negotiation, the in-between, the space of entre that Derrida has opened up in writing itself—that carries the burden of the meaning of culture . . . It makes it possible to begin . . . And by exploring this hybridity, this "Third Space," we may elude the politics of polarity and emerge as the others of ourselves. (Bhabha, "Cultural Diversity and Cultural Differences" 208–9)

In this space, then, identity can find language.

The construction of this "Third Space" is problematized by hegemony's affinity for legitimation, for legitimacy is necessarily constructed through historical claims of priority—that is, through origins. The adamistic desire for priority, patriarchy, and originality constructs mainstream culture, making it in consequence reluctant to acknowledge hybridity. In order to have voice—space, property, community—unadulterated claims must be "authenticated." Because this very process of authentication must take place within the vocabulary of hegemony, it will legitimate only that which conforms to its discursive field. Family—patriarchal and steeped in the declination of lineage and bloodlines—is the familiar trope of origins.

Minority subjectivity, with its relationships encoded outside property lines and established ancestral connection, finds no representation. Precisely because of this, minority discourse then must always struggle to undermine this system of origins, because within this larger system the subaltern cannot speak. The most familiar modes of disruption, noted with frequency by Bhabha, are mimicry, parody, and resistance. The instability this linguistic insurrection results in creates hybridity and the possibility of some new discursive space. Argues Bhabha: "Minority discourse sets the act of emergence in the antagonistic in-between of image and sign. . . . It contests genealogies of origin that lead to claims for cultural supremacy and historical priority. Minority discourse acknowledged the status of national culture—the people—as a contentious, performative space of perplexity" (*Nation* 307).

The discursive paradigm of hybridity finds, understandably, a great deal of articulation in the work of Native American critics. The problem of how to negotiate the problem of identity, when the very means of identity have been displaced by the western mechanisms of origins is central to this discussion. Chickasaw critic Jane Sequoya explores these constructs of identity in her essay, "How (!) is an Indian? A Contest of Stories." Sequoya maintains that, because "Indian-ness" is polyvocal and multiple, while hegemonic representation is necessarily singular, Native American identity is typically constructed along white lines. Indians are either represented as sentimental "artifacts"—"authentic" voices of nostalgia, or they are "outlaws" (165). Multicultural and multivoiced though they might be, the operatives of postcolonial power must cast them as subjects and represent their lives as "mechanical reproduction." No matter what the actuality of their lives, they will be represented within a fixed cultural grammar.

The result of this reductive process is that identity is made doubly difficult. Not only have Native Americans been stripped of their historic identities, but the very tools with which they are instructed to retrieve it—family trees, birth certificates, tribal rosters, land deeds, official documentation—are the civilizing instruments of the colonizing power:

> Institutions of capital define what it takes to be fully human in terms of those institutions—money and things—while the nostalgic system sees the Indian in terms of an imagined past . . . It is revealing of the problem for Native American identity in this contest of stories that Indian children who grew up with the genre of the American frontier movies identified with the cowboy heroes rather than with the Indian bad-guys; of course, Indians could not recognize themselves in the reflexive mirror held up by the popular media. (Sequoya 462)

Inhabitants of reservations are taught that their "Indian-ness," selfhood, and even survival are based upon their ability to produce and reproduce their origins for the appropriate agency. Emphasis is placed on biological lineage, rather than on communal connection. Minority identity then becomes an issue of hybridity, of exterior community discourse, of negotiation with and mimicry of the larger cultural vocabulary.

The process of this negotiation of Bhabha's "Third Space," within the context of the American continent and its historical discourse of race and blood is explored by critic Jean-Luc Nancy in his essay "Cut Throat Sun." Nancy traces the manner in which race and genealogical origins are traditionally understood in terms of "blood" ties and demonstrable genealogical connections. But these lines, Nancy reminds us, despite the American obsession with race (and hence with blood) are largely mythological; the identities of colonial and postcolonial subjects are constructed not through bloodlines but rather by "cuts." For Nancy, it is the sites wherein identity is ruptured and then, consequently, reconstructed that establish both individual and communal identity. The history of the American continent reveals torn familial patterns, the commingling of race, and a consciousness that is born not of continuity but of the rupture of continuities. Moreover, because these "cuts" refer not to a one-time historical event but instead to a cultural process, and because new "cuts" must necessarily occur, identity is no longer a subject that is fixed. An identity formed by the process of "cuts" is always in process. The "subject-in-process," contends Nancy, must "construct provisional identities" (135).[5]

The identity formed by "cuts" refutes traditional identities based upon genealogical exercises, bloodlines, or essentialisms regarding race. It is a subjective, mobile identity, concerned with the very act of cultural/familial/racial negotiation, rather than the notion of what cultures/families/races are being negotiated or blended. Says Nancy: "It [language, race] gets its identity from the cut, in the cuttings. It is no less an identification for it, but it is not an identity in terms of blood or essence. . . . Our naked existences: . . . interwoven . . . ill-woven . . . but woven one into the other. Sharing and crossing and bordering" (Nancy 117–18). For Nancy, hybridity—mixed blood—becomes the space of identity, and it is a space that destabalizes notions of origin. It is this temporarily occupied, ephemeral space of becoming that takes primacy over the mythic site of familial and blood origins.

It is toward an understanding and apprehension of this shifting "Third Space" and its constant displacement of genealogical origin that Erdrich's characters move. But, to do this they must confront the traditional vocabulary of blood. The hybrid space of nomadic and unstable terrain can only be discovered by demystifing the patriarchal web of familial and tribal origins, of language and, significantly, the underlying purpose of genealogy and family trees—property and capital.[6]

In *The Bingo Palace* this process of demystification involves a painful exploration of how the hegemonic codes of legitimacy and identity intersect the lives of her contemporary Chippewas. At the center of this exploration stands Shawnee Ray Toose, loved by both the novel's protagonist Lipsha and his older uncle/brother/cousin Lyman, who has a young son named, ironically, Redford.[7] As the most wealthy and seemingly powerful man on the reservation, Lyman has arranged for Shawnee Ray to live under his protection (and control), and claims Redford as his own son. Oppressed by her living situation, and divided in her affections, Shawnee Ray leaves the house and returns to her sisters' home. Using his influence, Lyman sends Officer Leo Pukwan (a despicable tribal henchman who has been emblematic of the corruption inherent in any constituted authority since his appearance in *Tracks*), a member of the tribal police, and a social worker, along with Lipsha's aunt Zelda, to retrieve the child. Pukwan and Zelda prove the legitimacy of the action with a search warrant, a court order, and the social worker's record of dependency:

"You've got no business here.". . . .
"We do have a warrant," said Pukwan evenly.
"And the court papers?"
"We've got those too," said Zelda. . . .
"Get the fuck out of here."
"We have papers," Zelda spoke emphatically.
"We're doing this for the protection of your nephew," said the social worker,
Vicki Koob, holding a manila envelope in the air. (174)

A short but violent altercation breaks out between Tammy Toose (Redford's maternal aunt) and the tribal police officer. Tammy is knocked unconscious with the officer's gun, and the screaming boy is driven away to be returned to Lyman; everything is done according to law.

The scene of Redford's removal, of course, parallels the historic treatment of Native Americans. Redford too is dispossessed, moved, and terrorized all for his own "protection," and his removal is legitimated by law. Moreover, Lyman's desire to possess the child is not fueled by his desire to provide more sanitary conditions for the youngsters of the reservation. Rather, he takes Redford as a hostage in his struggle to claim Shawnee Ray. Lyman, Chippewa though he may be, mimics the voice and vocabulary of white discourse.

But, embedded as he is within mainstream discourse, Lyman is insensitive to the nuances of hybridity. He believes that he will succeed because of his legitimized authority. Yet his control is ultimately subverted by Shawnee Ray who informs Lyman that she will vanish entirely if he ever repeats his authoritative performance. Lyman protests, and uses his assumed paternity to demonstrate his "rights" regarding the child. "'I'm Redford's father,' says Lyman gently" (188). But Shawnee Ray rebukes and makes foolish this claim, quickly dissolving Lyman's mythology of primacy of bloodlines: "You're too late. . . . Think back, Lyman," she warbles. "You weren't my only boyfriend, remember. I had three other guys, and I only made a birth control mistake with one of them. . . . Want to take a blood test?" (189). Confronted with the mystery of blood, Lyman retreats. "I'm messed up," he admits, for he is suddenly, confusedly aware of other more primal connection outside the laws, paperwork, and supposed family trees. To examine Redford's genealogy too closely is to disrupt the social order that Lyman has carefully erected.

The problems inherent in patriarchal discourse are made apparent much earlier in the Turtle Mountain novels. Fleur's ambiguous origins, which are sketched in *Tracks*, and the fate of June's violent, self-serving "legitimate" son, King, in *Love Medicine*, exemplify the ways in which the texts problematize familial legitimacy. Much of the earlier familial history concerns the way in which Lulu is removed from the community because there are no records establishing her paternity. Fleur is raped by three white men, and Lulu is the result. When Fleur vanishes, Lulu is sent to the Catholic Indian boarding school and disassociated from the reservation families. Lulu only can return when the older Nanapush becomes, by his own admission, a "bureaucrat" himself, aping the documents of paternity and claiming Lulu as his daughter. Lulu is returned because she possesses authenticated origins (and indeed, in chronologically later *Love Medicine*, we accept these fictional parental claims as true). The truth regarding Lulu's birth emerges, destablizing the claims of blood. Lulu ultimately, in *The Bingo Palace*, becomes a tribal chief, intent upon using the white man's law to enlarge and benefit the reservation.

Many other genealogical disturbances can be located in the texts, and these disturbances owe much to our Western desire to read for familial connections. Most readers of *Love Medicine* doubtless find it nearly irresistible to sketch family trees and connectives. In fact, much of what has been published in reference to Erdrich's novels performs this same function, endeavoring to clarify "the confusing jumble of characters" (*AIQ* 171). Critics have compared Erdrich's evocation of the Turtle Mountain Chippewa reservation to Faulkner's fictive Yoknapatawpha County. However, Erdrich's familial structures are complicated to the point of absurdity, for many of the characters "float" between families and trees, with a paternity that can never be established. June is simultaneously Gordon's sister, wife, and cousin. Lipsha claims Lyman as both brother and uncle, as well as rival in love. In places, the text suggests that both Fleur and June were fathered by the Manitous—the old, spirit ones, while Lulu's "real" paternity is accorded to three rapists.

Children move from one household to another, claiming each, briefly, as family. Marie Lazare we learn was never really a Lazare, and Lulu's many sons are all fathered by different men, allowing the legalistic claims of paternity to shift at whim. In fact, representation of parentless children who are absorbed into the larger community is a frequently repeated format. Fleur and her brother, aptly named Moses, wander one day onto the reservation land. They have no origins. In the same way, the protagonists of *The Beet Queen* simply appear one day in the community. June, and later, Lipsha are rescued from the lake that earlier threatened to claim Fleur. This trope finds particular resonance in a scene that occurs near the close of *The Bingo Palace*. Driving with his outlaw father, eluding the police, Lipsha and Gerry "accidentally" have a baby in their car with them. As Gerry leaves the car to follow the shade of June into the snow—and presumably into death—Lipsha rocks the infant who has now merged with his own earlier, lost identity, acknowledging that they are the same: "There is no trace where we were. Nor any arrows pointing to the place where we're headed. We are the trackless breast, the invisible light, the thought without a world to speak. Poured water, struck match. Before the nothing, we are the moment" (259). The lost baby, without origins and without direction, is the central metaphor of the text, a metaphor of "cuts" and nomadic displacement.

In Erdrich's work, the dead, the "originals," whom Western culture assumes should give their names and then disappear, are either nonexistent or they keep returning, thus confounding history and the status quo. History too is in this way destabilized, moving in and out of the present, leaving "tracks" that will keep altering the present. Thus, finally, paternity and the past are vehicles, not ways to remake the reservation in imitation of Anglo culture, but ways to decenter an assumed history. It is in the wake of this decentering that the community can shift and individuality can be discerned as a shifting hybrid state, rather than the static singular definition that culture would seem to demand.

In *The Bingo Palace*, genealogy, at least in the Anglo-European tradition, is revealed ultimately as the tool of property and capital. We erect our familial legacies so that we may inherit, and thus ensure that generational transition results in an uninterrupted stasis of power. To confuse legitimate genealogies then is tantamount to revolution. Erdrich's texts make this clear: Gerry the "illegitimate" activist son of Lulu, spends his life resisting the claims of the legitimate. He dispossess June's "legitimate" son King, defrauds the government, and removes a baby from its parent. But these acts possess a larger purpose. Gerry disrupts genealogy in order to improve the living conditions of his tribe. Like his mother Lulu, he seeks the return of lost Chippewa land.

"This Ain't Real Estate"

Land, or property—as it is termed within Western discourse—lies at the heart of genealogical debate, and Erdrich's tetralogy explores the interrelation between Western notions of property and its ultimate connection to identity. In *Tracks*, Lulu's mother Fleur Pillager struggles against a tide of forces who want to view her family place as property. As the only survivor of the tuberculosis epidemic in the early 1900s, Fleur takes possession of land granted her father under the Indian Allotment Act of 1904, which supplanted the infamous General Allotment (also known as the Dawes) Act of 1887. The Dawes Act called for the dissolution of reservation holdings through the granting of individual 160-acre allotments to male Native Americans over the age of 18. Under the modified act, "each enrolled member of the Turtle Mountain Chippewa born before 1909, received one quarter section of land, with single members of the tribe receiving lesser amounts" ("Fragmentation" 1). As for other tribes, the Dawes Act (and its variants) resulted in their dispossession of vast sums of Indian land. In her book *North American Indians*, Mary Jane Schneider points out that allotment policies immediately reduced total Indian land by sixty-five percent (1).[8]

But beyond the material consequences of allotment policies are the fundamental ideological shifts they perpetrated. Native Americans were encouraged to give up their "communism," and enter into the hegemonic vocabulary of private property, individualism, and authenticity. On the Turtle Mountain Chippewa reservation—as on other reservations—Indians were required to prove lineage and "authentic" connection to the tribe, before receiving allotments. Often tribe members were pitted against one another, or against outside agencies that wished to take possession of a particular plot of land. Often too, genealogical disputes erupted, or contentious debates developed over who would receive more valuable land assignments.

In *Tracks*, such tensions become apparent within the context of Erdrich's portrayal of the vying factions of the lumber company and neighbors who covet Fleur's land. Fleur's grandfather Nanapush observes the historical development of such policies, and their disruptive effect on his Turtle Mountain community. Coinciding with a terrible tuberculosis epidemic that further threatened tribal survival, allotment policies engendered a new lexicon of surveys, property, and possession: "In the past, some had sold their allotment land for one hundred poundweight of flour. Others, who were desperate to hold on, now urged that we get together and buy back our land, or at least pay tax and refuse the lumbering money that would sweep the marks of our boundaries off the map like a pattern of straws" (8). Ultimately, as old Nanapush relates, this new way of seeing land, as property, leads to further commerce and changed worldviews centered around capital. "Every year there are more who come looking for profit, who draw lines across the land with their strings and yellow flags," says Nanapush.

"They disappear sometimes, and now there are so many betting with sticks and dice out near Matchimanito at night, that you wonder how Fleur sleeps, or if she sleeps at all" (9). Thus the allotment policies, for Nanapush, like the yellow flags emergent on the landscape, signaled a historical shift in Chippewa conceptions of identity and community. These new conceptions were fueled by money and a desire for "legitimacy."

In *The Bingo Palace*, Erdrich amplifies this exploration of the hidden connections between genealogical-desire, legitimacy, and property. Much of the novel revolves around the site of Fleur's contested land. While in earlier texts/years the timber industry, as well as private Anglo individuals, struggled to divest Fleur of her holdings, in *The Bingo Palace* it is Lyman Lamartine, Lulu's "own" son (and thus a legitimate heir), who aspires toward ownership of the woods. Lyman dreams of a vast and ornate bingo palace, built on the land, which many consider sacred, from which he would reap huge sums of money. But Fleur is no more acquiescent than in earlier texts, resisting even as development moves forward. And when, toward the end of the novel, Lyman and Lipsha are driven to the woods on a vision quest, Fleur sends her familiar, a striped skunk, who repeats continuously, "This ain't no real estate." The land, suggests Fleur, no matter who owns it, no matter what the familial ties of inheritance, is not about private ownership and its conversion into commodity. There is, for Fleur and the text, a distinction between traditional land and real estate property.

Yet, Lipsha ponders, some use or cultivation of reservation land must take place, given the general level of poverty that exists on the Turtle Mountain reservation. The problem for Lipsha and indeed for the all of texts of the series is how to negotiate survivance without, finally, reducing individuality to mere commodification: "It's not completely one way or another, traditional against the bingo. You have to stay alive to keep your tradition alive and working" (221).

Lipsha attempts to focus upon the positive aspects of money and property, but he is haunted by the skunk. "This ain't real estate, it nags at me" (218). But it seems to Lipsha that the animal can only chant, providing no distinct answer. Lipsha ignores the skunk, but it persists. "Tell me something I don't know," requests Lipsha, and suddenly he is sent a vision:

The new casino starts out promising. I see the construction, the bulldozers scraping off wild growth from the land like a skin, raising mounds of dirt and twisted roots. Roads are built. . . . [it] is no longer a woods, as the building is set up and raised. It starts out as revenue falling out of the sky. I see clouds raining money in the open mouths of the tribal bank accounts. Easy money, easy flow. No sweat. No bother. I see money shining down like sunshine into Lyman Lamartine's life. It comes thick and furious. (219)

But the ecstasy fades; the vision quickly becomes troubled. Its glorious excess, neon flash, and capital have displaced "the lake that the lion man inhabits, where Pillagers drowned and lived" (219). The great dome that will hold the palace is revealed to be the giant shell of the turtle of the creation myth stories. As Lipsha contemplates further, he sees the members of his community intoxicated and held captive by "the perfect dreamstuff" of the large-screened bingo call letters. Disturbed, Lipsha argues with the skunk. He explains that he is lucky, that luck will bring "cash in my fingers." But the skunk speaks his last words. "Luck don't last when you sell it" (220). The "luck" of the traditional, that is, individual value, is corroded when it is sold.

Lyman's destiny exemplifies this corrosive process of commodification. Lipsha ponders how, even if there was "a great Native apocalypse," removing all of the Chippewa back "to the big shell that spawned us," "Lyman Lamartine's paperwork would live on, even flourish, for the types like him are snarled so deeply that they can't be pulled without unraveling bones and guts. Cabinets of files would shift priorities, regenerate in twice-as-thick reports" (197). Lyman has been reduced to a form, annihilated by the very mechanism of legitimacy that he celebrates. His faith in the language of capital, based as it is on genealogical legitimacy, is complete; for him there is no outside of the system. Co-opted, Lyman becomes part of the colonizing apparatus.

Ultimately, Lipsha concludes that there is no clear answer to the question of commodification. But he understands, as the text itself suggests, that to accept money for more than it is, and to fail to understand the nonmaterial meaning of land is a trap. To accept the arbitrary and meaningless letters of bingo as an alternate vocabulary is both vulgar and foolish. It has, argues the text, "no substance" (221). There is, however, an alternate vocabulary; this is the vocabulary that Fleur speaks, and that which Lipsha himself will have to come to understand as he moves toward "becoming."

It is, of course, not only the land that is commodified. Native American identity, faced with the American consumer's desire for the "authentic" and for historical origins, is made into a consumable fetish. *The Bingo Palace* traces this process, using Nector's tribal pipe as an example. As chief and tribal elder, Nector had a ceremonial pipe. Marie, living in a senior citizens' housing project, gives the pipe to Lipsha. She reminds him of the vocabulary of the pipe, "the old language in chunky phrases," and tells Lipsha that he will know how to use it. For Nector and Marie, the pipe was a way of accessing an alternate culture, the "Third Space" of Homi Bhabha. But Lipsha, at the moment he receives the gift, mistakes the pipe for something else, believing that it is a gesture of genealogy and familial acceptance. He is convinced that the gift legitimizes him finally as a family member. Shortly afterward, as Lipsha endeavors to cross the Canadian border for a dinner with Shawnee Ray, the pipe is commandeered by a custom's official. Reading the pipe from his own narrative—a narrative engendered by television Indians—the border official insists that the pipe is a hash pipe, and that Lipsha is in consequence a half-breed, drugged trouble-maker.

Rescued by his rival Lyman, Lipsha is forced to surrender the pipe, for Lyman demands it on both hereditary and economic grounds: "Nector Kashpaw was my real father. Goddamn it, Lipsha! Think about it once. Everybody could be getting inspirational from this pipe, it's a work of genuine art, it's spiritual. Only you'd rather keep it in your leaky trunk or stuffed in your footlocker. You don't deserve it!" (87). For Lyman, the pipe is both an object that can provide him with legitimation, and, simultaneously, an object—an artifact—of value. Illegitimate Lipsha can have no claim on what Lyman defines as an authentic and valuable artifact. Foolishly adapting Lyman's mode of thought, Lipsha offers to trade the pipe for Lyman's interest in Shawnee Ray (who is also Lyman's property because of his paternal interest in her son). Lyman immediately capitalizes on Lipsha's error. He threatens to tell Shawnee Ray of Lipsha's offer to buy her, a trick since Lipsha is actually the only one to even partially understand that love cannot be a commodity. Lyman keeps the pipe, but later falls victim to his own overwhelming gambling urge. He pawns the pipe for money. The pipe then provides a metaphor, allowing the reader to understand the ways in which genealogy, possession, and capital become entwined and displace any other conceptual worldview.

Just as corrosive, *The Bingo Palace* argues, is the residual effect this nexus of relations centered in genealogy, has on the very idea of ethical or equitable and loving relationships between people. In *The Bingo Palace*, commodification of women is tied to the notion of property, ownership, and agency, which is implicitly structured by Western patriarchal values. Erdrich's interrogation of patriarchal tendencies becomes quite clear in the respective cases of Lyman and Lipsha's mutual desire to possess Shawnee Ray. Like the pipe-artifact, or Fleur's land, Shawnee Ray, for Lyman, becomes yet another collectable. For Lyman, possession of Shawnee Ray has the power to grant him agency and identity as both patriarch and man.

In her representation of Lipsha's changing relation to Shawnee Ray, however, Erdrich provides readers a counter-narrative to Lyman's case. At first, with his new-found Bingo money, Lipsha believes he has gained power to win Shawnee Ray. Money provides him "insulation" in the form of possessions, which he believes will attract her. After purchasing from Lymann her "undivided attention" (95), however, Lipsha can only fantasize about her. Appropriately, he thinks of her metaphorically, as a precious commodity, an elusive object: "Yet the more I jump toward love the faster it flees. The more furious I throw my mental life into its capture, the more elusive it becomes. . . . No matter how hard I try, love is just beyond the tips of my fingers, precious as a field of diamonds and elusive, receding fast" (97). Shawnee Ray, of course, resists Lipsha, because what she initially valued in him was his carefree spirit, a sense that he too was an outsider, now displaced by his obsession to control her.

The unresolved relationship between Lipsha and Shawnee Ray is one of the more disturbing aspects of the novel, for it disrupts our Western notion of what "should" happen in a story. Since Lipsha is the mock "hero" of the novel, engaging and confused, devising his pursuit of the elusive Shawnee Ray, the reader expects, "desires" in Barthean terms, the successful culmination of the relationship. We want to see Lipsha settled and happy with Shawnee Ray and her son Redford, "shacked-up," as Lipsha puts it, in his new white Winnebago.[9] This traditional progression would allow the illegitimate Lipsha to be absorbed into a family; his romantic plight would be resolved and his identity and purpose made clear. It is indeed this end toward which Lipsha aspires. To this end, he plays bingo, hoping to win the prize van and capture Shawnee Ray: "[If] I won the van . . . there is a small refrigerator and a padded platform for sleeping. It is a starter home, a portable den with front-wheel drive, a place where I can shack with Shawnee Ray and her little boy. . . . I soon learn to be singleminded in my pursuit of the material object" (63).

But Lipsha's desire, as well as that of the reader, is frustrated. Shawnee Ray resists everyone's efforts—Lipsha's, Lyman's, and her Aunt Zelda's—to redefine her within a larger family structure. The text suggests that even romantic love has been tainted by the Western desire for family—genealogy—and ownership. To love, to marry, to give name to, and to produce children are gestures associated with this misplaced emphasis on bloodlines. Thus, Lipsha's professed "love" for Shawnee Ray is complicitious—

as is Lyman's authoritative affection—in a larger system of proprietary relations. As he attempts to command Shawnee Ray's love, Lipsha pleads
with her. "I've got the medicine," he boasts, referring to his mystical ability
to cure pain and provide sensuality. But Shawnee Ray rejects Lipsha, responding "You've got the medicine but you don't have the love" (151).

Desperate, Lipsha returns again to Fleur Pillager, mystical matriarch of
them all, for a potion or secret that will win Shawnee Ray. But Fleur laughs
at such simplicities, then shifts into an alternate shape and speaks to Lipsha
in a low, guttural language that he does not know but comes intuitively to
understand. In this language, outside the speech of postcolonialism, Fleur
is able to talk about love. But the words themselves, realizes Lipsha, cannot
finally be translated. She offers "no love teas, no dried frog hearts, no hints
or special charms" (151). Cryptically, Fleur communicates that love cannot
command, and that Lipsha must simply "accept" the pain of his love. Mys-
tified, Lipsha leaves her.

Significantly, it is the knowledge that love is about the self and can claim
no authority over the other that Lipsha must finally acknowledge. He must
eschew romantic possibility, for the way he has conceived of love is but a
manifestation of his cultural conditioning and colonial cultural production.
Painfully, Lipsha and the text argue that there must be some alternate perception of the self and its relation to others. Shawnee Ray leaves, forcing
Lipsha and the reader to a sort of epiphany: "My love before she [Shawnee
Ray] got so mad was all about what was best for Lipsha Morrissey . . . I have
reconsidered. If my love is worth anything, it will be larger than myself.
Which is not to say I don't dream about motels" (229–30). Lipsha continues in this vein, thinking of ways in which his affection could make him engage in good deeds of salvation in the tribal community. This epiphany
suggests that love, if it is really love and not concerned with familial lines
and possession, necessarily becomes reflexive with selflessness, and the
process of belonging to a community. At least for Lipsha and the Chippewa, love must be located outside the nexus of colonial culture. As Fleur's
speech carefully notes, even the actual vocabulary of love must be outside
Western discourse. "Love medicine" refers both to that language and to an
alternate sensibility. It is that mystical, traditional process that allows, at
least briefly, for the transcendence of a subjectivity (self) informed by colonial inscriptions.

This tension between desire and communal affection, between the lover
and the beloved, finds a similar articulation in the Turtle Mountain novels'
various couplings. The triangles of Lulu, Nector and Marie, June and

Gerry, and even Zelda and Xavier Toose provide examples of how love cannot be proprietary. Erdrich's women are not monogamous, nor is their culture patriarchal, but commodification provides increasing pressure on them to conform to the colonial model. The necessity to legitimate and fix familial relations, and to produce offspring who will further solidify and fix genealogical identity leads to the desire both to own the love object and to legitimate this ownership and propagation of offspring. Erdrich's text indicates that the pressure to conform to mainstream, genealogically legitimate, patriarchal culture results in the negation of the woman's in-process identity. Instead, she is a finite commodity. This becomes more than evident in Lyman's desire to possess Shawnee Ray and her son, and in the way he manipulates the paperwork of legitimacy. More disturbing is the way this same process nearly corrupts Lipsha's seemingly genuine love. He, too, translates love as possession, and struggles painfully to transcend the cultural model.[10]

It is significant that Lipsha's transcendence is never complete or everlasting, for it is the effort to negotiate the mobile nature of affection that moves Lipsha toward Bhabha's "Third Space." It is the "cuts" in Lipsha's relations with Shawnee Ray, his own uncertain heredity, and Raymond's unclear paternity that define both the text of the novel and the Turtle Mountain community. Lipsha does not simply travel from space to space and from identity to identity; instead, as he learns, he is always within the transient, nomadic space between. But for this space, there is no vocabulary and thus no means of representation. Lipsha's textual predicament is then doubly difficult; he must—as well as he can and frequently failing—represent the unrepresentable.

The difficulty of escaping from a vocabulary rooted in colonial discourse and Western patriarchy is noted by Nancy. Moreover, the cost of not escaping is that the colonial subject is constantly reduced to commodity. Every encounter with the colonial subject then becomes a confrontation with the Other, rather than any sort of communal exchange. Meditating on race, genealogy, and blood, and its tie to the economy of capital, Nancy remarks: "Today an unjustifiable, intolerable identity that is forced on us by the callous monster of technoeconomic necessity and the management or administration of this necessity. How to cut loose from it, what sort of revolution that would not be already outdated? Maybe that of the mestizaje . . ." (118). He says finally, that we must "relearn" the nature of cuts in order to understand the mobility of identity. Indeed, maintains Nancy, the history of the American continent is such, that it is a history about the "cutting" of race. This historic reality makes us all mestizo" (119). Resistance to the hardline of capital, multinational corporations, strategic downsizing and racial oppression requires a renewed resistance to the vocabulary of genealogy and the nostalgia associated with "blood."

And this of course brings us to the focus of Erdrich's text. By now it should be clear that *The Bingo Palace* provides a comprehensive critique of the relations that are structured genealogical desire and colonial forms of legitimacy. It is a novel of resistance. But questions arise: If "authenticity, patriarchy and blood," are connected to commodification, how do Native Americans escape the double-bind inherent in surviving within contemporary postcapital society? And returning to an earlier metaphor, what metaphoric path will allow Lipsha to sidestep or even subvert Western narratives of legitimacy and agency?

In *The Bingo Palace*, the answers to these questions are apparent in Erdrich's portrayal of alternate families—communities structured not so much by lineage and patriarchy, but rather through the development of a concept of love. For Erdrich, love emerges not so much as a romantic or physical construct but, rather, as a kind of subversive and healing force. *The Bingo Palace* and, in fact, the entire tetralogy are concerned finally in recementing the Chippewa understanding of community. Because all articulated ties are implicated in the process of colonial occupation, these relationships must be understood in alternate ways.

Indeed, this desire to redefine communal and familial relationships marks all of Erdrich's fiction, even where this theme is not, at least not overtly, the primary focus of the text. Erdrich's *Tales of Burning Love* (1996), a parodic novel distinctly different in tone from her earlier works, nonetheless deals with a community adjacent to the Chippewa reservation and provides a history and a future for some of her previous characters. It is the complicated legal and dynastic issues of these characters that form the center of this seemingly less complex text. In 1998, Erdrich published *The Antelope Wife*, a novel set in Minnesota, where the Ojibawa families settled in the vicinity of the Great Lakes. This novel, too, interrogates the by now familiar topics of history, mythology, tradition, and familial heritage. The novel's initial chapter opens with a scene of massacre, the rescue of a child, and a study of the miraculous, as a hardened soldier wills himself to mother and nurse a starving child. Through its tracery of ensuing relationships, *The Antelope Wife* suggests the difficulty in establishing history and "blood" bonds. Yet, still, the novel acknowledges the impossibility of utterly erasing these connections, suggesting that the lines between the literal and mythic must always be blurred.

But because Erdrich's texts are not naive, they suggest that a communal bond must, today, be carefully negotiated. To be part of such a community is to engage in the process of hybridity: it is to live within the larger, metaphorical bingo palace, wherein one stands simultaneously on sacred ground and on illusory cash; to be in the presence of both tradition and capitalism; and to play a game, wherein arbitrary letters and signs spell meaningless words that momentarily provide luck and legitimacy to the dispossessed.

Broken Worlds and Community

In *Migrancy, Culture and Identity*, Iain Chambers reminds us that the ideological and discursive forces that structure a sense of identity and community, founded on essentialist colonial notions of "authenticity," origins, and "blood," remains powerful. "In the idea of roots and cultural authenticity," writes Chambers, alluding to Benedict Anderson's *Imagined Communitites*, "there lies a fundamental, even fundamentalist, form of identity that invariably entwines with the nationalist myths in the creation of an 'imagined community'" (73). Yet out of the broken space of migrancy and such mobile communitites as the Turtle Mountain Chippewa, Chambers identifies a subversive prospect informed by history and lived experience. Out of the "broken world" of migrancy and colonialist intervention, a new world might emerge:

a world broken down into complexities, diverse bodies, memories, languages, histories, differences. The post-colonial presence, where the abstract metaphor of the "Other" is now metamorphosed into concrete, historical bodies, challenges the screen of universal thought—reason, theory, the West—that has historically masked the presence of a particular voice, sex, sexuality, ethnicity and history, and has only granted the "Other" a presence in order to confirm its own premises (and prejudices). (70)

Emerging from the subversive and discontinuous space of such "broken worlds," Erdrich's texts compose a ruse. Like the miscellaneous letters of the bingo game, names and stories suggest a meaningful connection, spelling, in this case, family rather than bingo. But just as the bingo signs are essentially meaningless, providing a prize only by virtue of the community's consent, the cult of family connections spell out an empty word. Genealogy is a learned aspect of colonial culture, like the bingo game imported by the missionaries. If the arbitrariness of these signs is not recognized, they will come to displace the more pressing, historic, and visceral demands of community. Accepted simply as a learned speech to be used in certain material dialogues with the dominant culture, the signs are just games. And it is in between these subtle games that contemporary Native American identity must be forged, in a hybrid gaming of alternate languages and the disturbing knowledge that there is no "authenticity," only the mutual need and play of a vital community.

Notes

1. In April 1996, Erdrich published *Tales of Burning Love* (New York: Harper Collins). While this novel is located in a town nearly adjacent to the Turtle Mountain reservation and concerns a few of the characters introduced in earlier novels, it is not considered a formal segment of her series. However, the novel does engage issues of paternity. Jack, the novel's sometimes narrator must acknowledge that his child—"my son"—can belong to a lesbian couple.

2. Erdrich suggests that writing history is, for Native Americans, an exercise in identity, for the history of American Indians is one of rupture. In consequence, identity is also ruptured. Native American writers, argues Erdich, "have therefore a task quite different from that of other writers." They are writing after the apocalypse, after the "unthinkable has already happened." What is therefore required is a new lexicon (*New York Times Book Review*, July 28, 1985).

3. The history of the Chippewa Nation reflects a nomadic subject position. Pushed from the territory of the Great Lakes region, the Chippewa were interned in the vastly different and seemingly un-homelike regions of South Dakota.

4. While few critics have commented on the resemblance Gerry bears to activist Leonard Peltier, the comparison seems obvious. Like Peltier, Gerry is an activist who seeks asylum in Canada and is imprisoned for a murder he insists that he did not commit. Just as Peltier's case is haunted by the vague picture of "Mr. X," Gerry's relatives insist that they know the "real" truth behind the murders. Information regarding Peltier can be found in Peter Mathiessen's *In the Spirit of Crazy Horse* (Viking Penguin, 1991), as well as in Dee Brown's *Bury My Heart at Wounded Knee* (Holt, Rinehart & Winston, 1970).

5. For a further discussion of this "tactical subjectivity," see Chela Sandoval's "U.S. Third World Feminism: The Theory and Method of Oppositional Consciousness in the Postmodern World," *Genders*, spring, 1991.

6. The discussion of origins is pivotal to postmodern discourse. Gilles Deleuze and Felix Guattari's seminal study, *Anti-Oedipus: Capitalism and Schizophrenia* (University of Minnesota Press, 1983), provides a clear depiction of how the desire for the "genesis of the machine" and the act of production figures into the Western desire for stable origins. Deleuze and Guattari argue that this totalizing focus on the moment of production is an attribute of capitalism and machine culture. Further, they contend that conventional psychoanalysis is based on this notion of genesis, both the genesis of production and the genesis of pathology. Analysts hold their patients stationary on the couch and attempt to move them back to their psychoanalytic and sexual origins. But, the "schizophrenic," the individual who is outside patriarchy and capitalism, is a nomad who would rather be "out for a walk" amid the

"deterriorialized flows of desire, the flows that have not been reduced to the Oedipal codes . . . and the desiring machines."

7. Redford's name is of course a kind of semiotic play. He is indeed "red"—that is, Native American. Further, his redness is something that must be forded, crossed and negotiated. But his name is also a reference to Robert Redford, the blond, movie star ideal who represents the Anglo, "All-American" male. Robert Redford is a role toward which Redford can only aspire; he can never be the ideal defined by his name.

8. The history of land deals and the resultant dispossession has been documented in numerous places and could fill many volumes. The Allotment Acts, despite their name, were part of a systematic dissolution of reservation lands. These acts used genealogy and Native Americans' traditional lack of paper documentation as a means of dispossession. The end result of these Allotment Acts was that reservation land decreased and that Indians were forced to become absorbed in the legal systems of genealogy that structure conventional discourse. For a further discussion see Schneider's work, as well as Vine Deloria's *Custer Died for Your Sins* (Norman: University of Oklahoma Press, 1970).

9. Cars are highly significant in Erdrich's tetralogy. They represent the space between and the nomadic, mobile natures of their drivers. Most of the vehicles utilized by Erdrich also reference Chippewa and, more generally, Native American mythologies. *Love Medicine* charts the passage of the Firebird, a care that houses June's spirit and moves Gerry toward freedom and Lipsha nearer understanding. The Winnebago is, of course, associated with the trickster god. Interestingly enough, most Winnebagos that one sees on the road bear names like "The Brave" or "The Warrior." The issue of cars in Erdrich is addressed by Marvin Magalaner in his essay "Of Cars, Time and the River," *American Women Writing Fiction: Memory, Identity, Family, Space* (ed. Mickey Pearlman, University of Kentucky Press, 1989).

10. Paula Gunn Allen addresses the problem of the commodification of women within the larger system of patriarchy in her text *The Sacred Hoop: Recovering the Feminine in American Indian Traditions* She suggests that the colonial models have brought a particular pressure to bear on American Indian women, and that this model must be resisted. Her argument is a kindred piece to Erdrich's novel.

Works Cited

Bhabha, Homi, K. *Nation and Narration*. London: Routledge, 1990.
——. "Post-Colonial Criticism," *Redrawing the Boundaries*, eds. Stephen Greenblatt and Giles Gunn. New York: Modern Language Association of America, 1992.
——. "Cultural Diversity and Cultural Differences," *The Post-Colonial Studies Reader*, ed. Bill Ashcroft. London: Routledge, 1995.
Bruchac, Joeseph. "Whatever Is Really Yours: An Interview with Louise Erdrich," *Survival this Way: Interviews with American Indian Poets*. Tucson: University of Arizona Press, 1987.
Chambers, Iain. *Migrancy Culture Identity*. London: Routledge, 1994.
Deleuze, Giles, and Felix Guattari. *Anti-Oedipus*. Minneapolis: University of Minnesota Press, 1983.
Erdrich, Louise. *Love Medicine*. New York: Bantam, 1985.

——. *The Beet Queen*. New York: Bantam, 1986.

——. *Tracks*. New York: Harper, 1988.

——. "A Writer's Sense of Place," *A Place of Sense: Essays in Search of the Midwest*, ed. Michael Marton. Iowa City: University of Iowa Press, 1988.

——. *The Bingo Palace*. New York: HarperCollins, 1994.

Tales of Burning Love. New York: HarperCollins, 1996.

The Antelope Wife. New York: HarperCollins, 1998.

Larson, Sidner. "The Fragmentation of a Tribal People in Louise Erdrich's *Tracks*." *American Indian Culture and Research Journal* 17:2 (1993) 1–13.

Maristuen-Rodakowski, Julie. "The Turtle Mountain Reservation in North Dakota: Its History as Depicted in Louise Erdrich's *Love Medicine* and *Beet Queen*," *American Indian Culture and Research Journal* 12:3 (1988) 33–48.

Nancy, Jean-Luc. "Cut-Throat Sun," *An Other Tongue*, ed. Alfred Arteaga. Durham: Duke University Press, 1994.

Schneider, Mary Jane. *American Indians*. Dubuque: Kendali Publishing, 1986.

Sequoya, Jana. "How (!) Is and Indian?: A Contest of Stories," *New Voices in Native American Criticism*, ed. Arnold Krupat. Washington: Smithsonian Institution Press, 1993.

CHAPTER SEVEN

In the Shadow of the Crazies: The Omnipresent Father and Thomas McGuane's Deadrock Novels

"Are we lost?" —Thomas McGuane, *Nothing but Blue Skies*

Hidebound Mythologies

IN HIS CENTENNIAL anthology of Montana writers, *The Last Best Place* (1988), William Kittredge contends that the Montana school of contemporary writers has managed to diverge from "the old hidebound mythology of the West." These Montana authors, contends Kittredge, create an alternative West both by "defining their own demons and battles," thereby critiquing the frontier's patriarchal landscape, and by engaging in the "constant business of the artist—renaming the sacred" (760). For Kittredge, this process involves discovering or rediscovering "the possibility of a coherent life in the last best place" (765).[1]

For Montana's contemporary writers—as for other contemporary writers of the West—the "possibility of a coherent life" is undeniably complicated by the problematic demons from a discursive past that seems to extend to the very landscape itself. In the works of such writers as James Welch, Thomas McGuane, Jim Harrison, Richard Ford, and James Crumley, the past is less a distant referent than a painfully pervasive presence. Like the sharp rises of the Crazy Mountains or the verdant, pastured expanses of the butte flatlands, it seems an indelible feature of the landscape. Within the land of Montana itself, the violent mythologies of the past seem quite literally to reside beneath its very surface in the many military silos that lie across Montana. Beyond marking old cold war tensions, the nuclear missiles of Montana suggest a kind of apotheosis of the violence that characterizes the masculine codings of the Old West, the legacy of a "gun-fighter nation." And yet, it is precisely to this conflicted land above the silos that contemporary Americans have fled in record numbers. And it is this environment to which advertisers turn when attempting to associate a product with some naturalized version of an earlier idyllic America.[2] The contemporary Montana explored by these writers thus represents a kind of contradiction. At once the resonant site of some indelible and hopelessly nostalgic past, the West emerges simultaneously as a site of danger, a place where if "a man's got to do, what a man's got to do," the consequences may be cataclysmic.

Perhaps more than any other place, the Montana territory has been defined as a space of national theater; it serves as a panoramic auditorium, where the drama of "American frontier history" can be perpetually staged. It is where the contradictions inherent in western mythologies are reified and subverted. It is a space historically dominated by masculine constructions and marked by the patriarchal mission of manifest destiny. It is the scene of the virgin land permanently occupied and claimed by the father. Critic Homi Bhabba maintains that the space defined by nationalist mythology necessarily remains engaged with a discourse that is patriarchal and phallic. The edifice of the father dominates this conversation, insists Bhabba, casting an eerie shadow across the cultural landscape. This same shadow marks the Montana territory—the grassy flatlands and the jagged peaks of the well-named Crazy Mountains.

But the father is not a benevolent, gentle father, nor are his offspring "good" sons. The father seeks to control and the sons seek to wrest control; this is the necessary hierarchy of the conquered and colonial space. Violence, rupture, and discord must inevitably define relations that are thereby always dangerous. Insurgence is continual, and threat and instability become tropes of the larger topography. Thus, argues Bhabba in "The Other Question: Difference, Discrimination and the Discourse of Colonialism," "the American border as a cultural signifier of a pioneering, male 'American' spirit [is] always under threat" (74). The result is certain violence and the construction of a father who is deeply problematic. As the West is the final territory of the father, it must share the paternal legacy—painful, dysfunctional, and irretrievably conflicted.

It is this troubled legacy that haunts twentieth-century western writers and Montana authors in particular. The suicide of author Richard Brautigan marks the cost exacted by the territory. Nonetheless, these (male) writers are still seduced by the lure of Montana and the lurid promotion of the west—a lure based on the mass-produced vision of a rugged man hunting, fishing, trapping, tramping, riding, and simply being alone with himself. Far from naive, and critical of the nationalistic literature that has come to define the genre of the western, these contemporary writers situate themselves as new, younger, and more willful sons. Their desire is to undermine the father—in both a political and literary sense.

But they are only partially successful. For if, as Bhabba claims, "the death of the father is the intervention on which [new] narrative is initiated," the absence of the father results in the creation of a similar and restorative narrative which inevitably struggles to restore the structure of patriarchy. The son becomes the father, and then future sons undermine him. It is difficult to erase the conceptual father from within the confines of the patriarchal space. This dilemma is apparent in the writing of contemporary Montana authors; their writing is as conflicted as the territory they inhabit. These authors critique the western construction of masculinity, yet the same construction continually corrals their own fiction.

Amid the contemporary scene, perhaps no author is so associated with present-day Montana as Thomas McGuane. McGuane's Deadrock novels-—*Nobody's Angel* (1982), *Something to Be Desired* (1984), *Keep the Change* (1989), *Nothing but Blue Skies* (1992)—all geographically situated in the fictional town of Deadrock, Montana, represent a ceaseless project by McGuane to interrogate the legacy of the West and its impact on American culture. Indeed, all examine the reflexive relationship between the discourse of the mythic western and masculine identity. While they invoke the tropes of the typical westerns in the process, McGuane's Deadrock scenarios are often comically ironic. His protagonists, though more or less cowboys, are self-conscious about the mythic coding of the frontier. As unenthusiastic inheritors of a mythic identity, they seem to exist in some space between the discursive West and the "real" West.

Indeed, questions involving an inherited "mythic identity," at once violent and nostalgic, and the construction of masculine identity within the context of these forces, form the central thematic concerns of McGuane's Deadrock novels. For McGuane, Deadrock provides a resonant site from which to critique the western rugged individualism, handed down by such historic fathers as Frederick Jackson Turner, in which the frontier trope serves as a repository for a particular American nationalistic identity founded on patriarchy and phallocentric mastery of the wilderness space.

In particular, McGuane's fiction can be seen to examine what Homi Bhabha has called the "Father's absence presence," with relation to frontier constructions of masculinity, and its connections to the old "hidebound" mythologies.[3] For McGuane, this comic deconstruction involves the exploration of some familiar western tropes that seem in many ways to have "come with the territory." McGuane exposes the strong patriarchal fathers of the West and explores their violent western legacies. His novels interrogate the semiotics of the frontier. And as McGuane probes the sacred ritual of trout fishing, he moves deep within the mythic constructions of masculinity in the west.

Fathers and Sons

Nobody's Angel, the first of McGuane's Deadrock novels, begins with an image that will remain a specter throughout the Deadrock novels. His disillusioned protagonist, Patrick Fitzpatrick, finds he can't escape the haunting image of his dead father. A test pilot for Boeing, Patrick's father had died the year before in a spectacular airplane crash amid the vertiginous recesses of the Crazy Mountains.[4] Eventually, in the dark of winter, Patrick ventures by horseback into the ice-scaped Crazies and discovers in the milky vagueness of the sheet ice the frozen form of his dead father: "Unable to differentiate flesh and electronics, [Patrick] was avoiding the longheld notion that his father had died like a comet, igniting in the atmosphere, an archangelic semaphore more dignified than death itself. For Patrick, a year had begun. The inside of the lane showed him that life doesn't just always drag on" (5–6). As McGuane's vivid description signals, for young Patrick—"a fourth generation cowboy outsider, and educated man, a whiskey addict and until recently a professional soldier"—finding his father literally inscribed on his beloved landscape represents something more than a lasting legacy (4).

Patrick's father's fusion with the landscape of the Crazy Mountains implicitly serves to memorialize an atavistic vision of life in the "Old West" that Patrick can't abide, yet must constantly negotiate. As a soldier, horseman, and alcoholic, returned home to Montana to try to work the ranch and look after his grandfather, Patrick suffers terrible bouts of "sadness for no reason." He feels tormented by his still psychically powerful, if absent, father.

Like other Deadrock protagonists, Patrick is a figure inextricably caught between the "real" West and the discursive West, a West produced by centuries of cultural production extolling fantasies of the "rugged frontiersman," of what it "means to be a man" in the harsh environs of the American west. And even though Patrick is self-conscious about the "constructed-ness" of these fantasies from the past, he nonetheless can't seem to escape their hold. "Patrick felt that in fact there had been a past," writes McGuane," but only that it was so broad he could not discover its curves, the ones that propelled him into the present, or glory or death" (63). For Patrick, his doomed sense of "sadness-for-no-reason" emerges as the result of his strange acculturation in the ever-mediated West. Unable to discover anything quite genuine, he floats. Indeed, the resonant image haunting *Nobody's Angel* is of Patrick floating in the ethereal blackness of unnamed rivers. He drifts amid stories of his tough father and cowboy grandfather, amid stories from Deadrock's illustrious history and its significance in the West, amid stories of wars and conquests, and of what it means to be a western hero.

Like other Deadrock men, Patrick suffers profoundly from the stories that seem to prefigure not only his own life, but those of generations before him. In *West of Everything* Jane Tompkins comments that the discursive terrain of the generic western developed in the nineteenth century in reaction to the rising tide of sentimentalism, engendered by such "women's novels" as Warner's *The Wide, Wide World* (1850) and Stowe's *The Minister's Wooing* (1859) (38). As forms of cultural production emergent within the reactionary "cult of masculinity" in nineteenth-century America, westerns and frontier narratives asserted overtly phallocentric fictional worlds in opposition to the Christianized worlds of sentimental fiction. For Tompkins, this discursive paradigm and its inevitable phallocentric and violent itinerary, symbolized by struggles between rivals and fights to "death with guns," deeply involves itself both in perpetuating and preserving a western mythos of masculine identity (38). "The Western doesn't have anything to do with the West as such," writes Tompkins, "It isn't about the encounter between civilization and the frontier. It is about men's fear of losing their mastery, and hence their identity, both of which the Western tirelessly reinvents" (45).[5]

As an enunciative cultural text, Frederick Jackson's Turner's "The Significance of the Frontier in American History" speech, at the Chicago Exposition of 1893, certainly stands out as a moment when the relationship between identity, mastery, and the frontier was reinvented. As discussed elsewhere in this text, Turner's well-known thesis projected an American identity founded on the exclusion of Others and the ascendancy of a particular American character forged by the frontier. Turner's American colonist represented a "composite nationality," who had achieved, through violent confrontation with the wilderness, a "masterful grasp of material things." He had gained a particular kind of masculine identity, which, as the frontier margin disappeared, was threatened. For Turner, "the dominant traits of the nation—strength and inventiveness of mind, buoyancy, and exuberance of spirit, 'restless, nervous energy,' and a 'dominant individualism'—were the 'traits of the frontier, or traits called out elsewhere' because of the existence of the frontier" (*Cultural* 28). These were the traits of the mythological father.

This implied relationship between "dominant individualism" and a projected national character in Turner comes into focus when we consider Homi Bhabha's comments on the construction of masculinity and its relation to patriarchy. As Bhabha asserts, the discourse of masculinity "is a discourse of self-generation, reproduced over the generations in patrilineal perpetuity" that "seeks to make a name for itself" (57). It emanates from narratives of nationalism:

The arbiter of this nationalist/naturalist ethic is the bearer of a peculiar, visible invisibility (some call it the phallus)—the familial patriarch. The position must be understood as an enunciative site—rather than an identity—whose identification axes can be gendered in a range of strategic ways. The instinct for respect—central to the civic responsibility for the service of nation-building—comes from father's sternness. (59)

For Bhabha, the "phallic peripherality" inherent in implied hierarchies of nationalism thus are reflected and enunciated in "father's sternness" and his position as patriarch. Turner's vision of a particular frontier "identity," reflexive with certain "national characteristics," in turn corresponds precisely to Bhabha's "self-generated discourse" and its dissemination in "patrilineal perpetuity." Indeed, Turner's elegiac speech is cautionary—the fatherly reiteration of the importance of the "old hidebound mythologies." But beyond, it reflects the degree to which the sign of the father is indelibly linked to a phallocentric coding of masculinity, which has resonances with the dysfunctional world McGuane explores.

As presaged by the disturbing image of Patrick's dead father in *Something to be Desired*, all of McGuane's Deadrock novels self-critically examine the problematic nature of this discursive "western" identity handed down by fathers. For McGuane, this dysfunction associated with the western father's handing down a mythos of "rugged individualism," invariably emerges within the context of family settings. Indeed, just as Bhabha suggests, the family becomes the place where such corrosive patriarchal myths of western masculinity and ideas of nationalism find expression. It is through the western narrative that these myths are reified and bequeathed from fathers to sons. In *Something to Be Desired*, for example, this mechanism of inheritance is established. The narrative opens by establishing a formative event experienced by young Lucien, who will struggle to achieve self-awareness as an adult. As a child, Lucien travels with his father into the Crazies on a camping trip. The scene begins idyllically enough, invoking a semiotics of romance in which the moon "lofted off the horizon" as Lucien, in a baseball uniform, walks beside his father (3).

Soon, however, the scene shifts, slipping into dystopic dread. Readers confront images that counter the idyllic codings. We learn that Lucien and his father hide from Lucien's mother in "of all places, Arequipa, Peru, where he had cooked on sheep dung and drunk too much and mailed deranged letters to his son until his son flunked his courses and got kicked off the baseball team" (4). Correspondingly, after their forced return to the States, Lucien and his father become lost in the Crazy Mountains, a locale that establishes an emblematic metaphor for the larger cultural condition of Deadrock men who all struggle with the historic masculinized codings of the West.

Although Lucien comes to deplore his father's romantic escapades, he nonetheless is compelled to repeat them. Growing up, Lucien becomes obsessed with such rugged heroes as Ernest Thompson Seton and Theodore Roosevelt. Later, he works his way through college as a log-choker, tool-pusher, fencer, irrigator, and cowboy. Ultimately, he too escapes to South America, having had a child by a wife who has left him. When he returns home to Montana, where he ultimately begins to confront himself, he spends much of his time drunk. Following one of his "blackouts," he unwittingly awakes in a hotel appropriately called the El Western, an experience to which his absent father would have doubtless related to.

The looming father figure—as sign of the West, as dysfunctional, as violent and powerfully prefigurative, the father as defined by Bhabba—appears in slightly different forms in both *Keep the Change* and *Something to Be Desired*. Though less flamboyant than Lucien's father, Joe Starling's father in *Keep the Change* similarly casts a seemingly inescapable shadow. Again, the novel begins with an evocative and illustrative father-son tableau. Here we find artistically inclined young Joe Starling on a trip with his father to inspect the failing family ranch. Joe's father has recently had a change of fortune and is coming to terms with the idea of giving up the western life. Already overabsorbed in business, the older Starling has come to accept that the western life can't support him. As he admits to Joe, "I wish I could have found a way of staying in this country. . . . But any fool can see it's going nowhere . . . , it's time to whistle up the dogs and piss on the fire" (11).

Frank Copenhaver, in McGuane's most recent Deadrock installment *Nothing but Blue Skies*, must also struggle with the problematic legacy of his father. In this version of the "cold blooded westerner," the father figure is less a cowboy than a ruthless businessman. Frank, who comes of age in the sixties, ultimately can't abide his father's hard-nosed ideas and inability to "trust anyone" (149). Nonetheless, he can't seem to escape the power of the man and is "overpowered by fear of his father. He felt his drugged and drunken vagueness in fuzzy contrast to his father's forceful clarity next to him, a presence formed by a life time of unstinting forward movement, of farming, warfare and freemarket capitalism as found in a small Montana city" (7). Like both Joe and Lucien, Frank's life dissolves into a series of cataclysmic events in which he struggles to understand his own life against his father's. His father's power, however, proves inescapable in terms of Frank's own problematic trajectory. When his wife Gracie leaves him, because he has begun to exhibit a "take-no-prisoners" (ruggedly individualistic) attitude in business, Frank is forced to reevaluate his relationship with his father, as well as the rest of his family.

For all of McGuane's Deadrock protagonists, it is the family and relationships that ultimately become the site of these paternal conflicts. As troubled, world-weary children of Turnerian individualists, they have inherited a West that seems irresolutely destructive to family. Indeed, here in reconstructed frontier of Deadrock, business and interpersonal spheres seem to have replaced the mythic saloon or high-noon showdown. As such, McGuane's world represents the recoding of the "old hidebound myths" within the postmodern context of our commodified culture. Patriarchal mastery and its violent enunciation in business are thus the legacy of Turner's composite American.

Deadrock Woman

If, in 1893, Turner's iconic "frontier hypothesis" erroneously projected the American West as a geography devoid of women, Indians, Mexicans, and African Americans, it nonetheless established a prevailing mythic context in which "real" westerners "were innovators in material things, were impatient of restraint, and were highly nationalistic" (235). The interconnection between a sense of Anglo-American national identity, and the monochromatic West as posited by Turner and neo-Turnerians, correspondingly becomes a point of interrogation for McGuane. McGuane's Deadrock plays with the legacy of phallocentrism and a monochromatic view of the West, but his "imagined community," to borrow Benedict Anderson's phrase, is rather a site of ironic ruptures, and decentered mastery; a place where Others have resisted the hegemonic forces that have attempted to elide their presence. Indeed, most often, the rupturing of the Turnerian masculanist model occurs when Others find voice in Deadrock and figuratively disrupt the monologues of men. (The very name of Deadrock is, of course, emblematic. As opposed to bedrock—a space of origins—Deadrock references the inert, calcified, and even toxic, as well as the cliché of the western town.)

Thus, besides emerging as a landscape haunted by rugged fathers and their communities, Deadrock proves notable for its Others—most often women—who serve to destabalize and problematize the concept of a "masculine" and phallocentric west. The Deadrock protagonists all struggle to hold onto mythic, heroic, western behavior, only to be undermined by women. Indeed, if McGuane's protagonists suffer from a problematic masculine identity engendered by their Turnerian fathers, it is the Deadrock women who most often provide insights into the disturbing phenomena. Humorously decentering depictions of the West as the "white" man's domain, these women more often than not are ultimately more individualistic and self-reliant than their male counterparts. As such, they ironically subvert mythological expectations and provide a critique of a "historic west" without Others, and suggest how McGuane's highly ironic West actually engages in a postmodern critique of representation. This resistance by the feminine Other is noted by Bhabha in his examination of patriarchy. The gendering of national character simultaneously engenders definition and agency of the Other, creating "an understanding of subaltern agency as the power to reinscribe and relocate the given symbols of authority and victimage" ("Man" 64).

In *Nothing but Blue Skies*, for example, Gracie understands Frank's neurosis as an overcompetitive obsession inherited from his father. Her own interests—cooking, growing herbs, hiking—have been consumed by Frank's monomaniacal desire to "own-it-all," to in a sense eclipse his father as a rancher/businessman. In the course of their marriage, she has seen Frank evolve into a hybrid Turnerian, virtually disavowing his "hippie," counterculture past. As she tells him: "I always was able to stand it, able to stand you making fun of my dopey little restaurant, able to watch the side of your head buried in the Wall Street Journal, even though it was the same head that was once buried in Carlos Castaneda, the I Ching, Baba Ram Dass. . . . because you had such a wonderful relationship with Holly [their daughter]. . . . But then, it seems unbelievable, Holly grew up and left. And I couldn't lie to myself anymore" (346). When she decides to leave Frank, she carefully, shrewdly, assesses the condition of their lives, and decides it has been all but irrevocably poisoned by Frank's craziness.

Nothing but Blue Skies opens at the moment of dissolution. Frank can be seen desperately trying to reinvent himself as a kind of caricature of western masculinity. Deciding to get on with his life without Gracie, and in an effort to impress his new romantic interest, Gracie's ex-best friend Lucy, he enlists in an ill-advised trip to the North Pole. For Frank, the trip promises a chance to remasculinize himself, but as it unfolds, it dissolves into a parody of the picaresque hero-quest. In the frigid inclines, nothing goes as it should. The Inuit he meets, thoroughly eccentric, self-directed and "human," ruptures his fantasy.

Gracie, by contrast, functions as an isolate. Her resourcefulness ironically places her in a much better financial position than Frank. Once back home, Frank thus pines for Gracie, not merely for her return and a hoped for reconciliation, but because he realizes that she in fact is much more noble, heroic, and honorable than he. Initially blaming her for his failures, Frank comes to reevaluate his own priorities and understand Gracie's "abandonment" as a courageous departure.

Towards the novel's conclusion, Frank has an epiphany. Obsessing on Gracie's telling "monologue," which she delivered to him as a way of explaining why she was leaving him, Frank ponders her claim that he had made her feel "invisible." Thinking about it, "he wanted some sense he wasn't falling into the hole he felt opening in the middle of himself. He tried imagining a time in the future when they were all gone and none of this mattered. And it didn't help. Gracie once accused him of making her feel invisible. What if Holly [his daughter] had said, "you made my mother invisible" (346). Gracie's claim of being "invisible" within Frank's world, and within Deadrock itself, alludes to Turner's forgotten Others. In this masculine site—where ranch life has slipped irrevocably into *mano-y-mano* business deals and zealous competitiveness, Gracie's emergence as a viable, independent woman suggests an awakening on Frank's part. Not only does Gracie—as woman, as Other—have legitimacy within this historically resonant landscape, but her personal style and courage strike

Frank as ultimately more viable and worthwhile than his own myopic, corrosive vision. In her own way, Gracie manages to rupture Frank's consciousness and his acculturation into the ways of the masculine West.

In McGuane's earlier Deadrock novels, such hopeful realizations are not as vivid, but they are nonetheless present. *In Keep the Change*, for example, the women who share the narrative focus with Joe Starling—his two "lovers" Astrid and Ellen, and his Aunt Lureen—demonstrate much more strength and resiliency in confronting the shifting West than does Joe. His Aunt Lureen suffers heroically the alcoholic binges of Uncle Smitty, whose get-rich-quick entrepreneur's schemes and fantasies of escape ultimately lead him to jeopardize the family ranch. As the true "provider" and preserver of the homestead, Lureen combines a rugged individuality with an abiding love for Smitty—in spite of the absurdity of his wild ideas and ill-conceived plans. Rather than acting as the silent partner in ranch duties, reflective of the "silent" and "strong" type of woman that forms the basis for traditional hegemonic discourse of the frontier, Lureen is the functional head of the household.

Both Starling's lovers, Astrid and Ellen, also resist the stereotypical categories associated with "frontier women." When Joe childishly "kidnaps" Ellen, she quite directly and astutely disabuses him of his foolish notions regarding their relationship. She explains to Joe that their relational mishaps were resultant from his blindly treating her as a "type"—another woman—while her husband, Billy, actually saw "who" she was. Preferring, finally, Billy's knowledge, she tells Joe, "Billy knows everything there is to know about me, and he loves me" (218). Ellen's comments make Joe realize that "she had a point. It was about lives that were specific to each other. It wasn't about generalities. It wasn't about 'love.' 'Love' was like 'home'" (218). Joe's "masculine" behaviors—tropes instigated in the west—are revealed to be empty rhetoric.

Astrid similarly subverts Joe's expectations, and provides a perspective against which Joe can measure not only his own foolish notions about masculinity—inherited from his father—but perhaps more importantly, his skewed, destructive attitude toward art. When Astrid shows up in Deadrock, following Joe's flight, she clearly arrives as a free agent. Like Gracie, she resists dependency. A Latina, Astrid is referred to by some in town as the "Mexican woman" staying with Joe. But as an outsider, she remains coolly aloof, derailing the preconceived notions about her. Ultimately, Joe admires Astrid for these strengths, and any sense of hope develops out of her "wisdom."

In the final moments of the novel, Joe indeed begins to question his entire western existence. He thinks back to his father cleaning grouse, and remembers his father's comment: "I wish I was a vegetarian. You never have to pick number-eight shot out of a tomato!" (230). Joe's memory is ironic—pointing to a new understanding that perhaps his father's fate as a "man of the West" had been as prefashioned as his own, and that this identity was violent and consuming. Appropriately, the novel ends with a clearing sky and thoughts of Astrid, who had been partially responsible for Joe's changing perceptions: "The sky was blue and the air coming from under the slightly opened window so cold and clean that he admitted to himself that his spirits were starting to soar. He thought he'd begin to get his things together. He stood in the window a moment more and looked out at the beautiful white hills. What Astrid had said, more or less, was that they would pretty much have to see" (230). Joe's recognition of both his own foolishness and Astrid's intelligence—and agency—ends the story, suggesting that Joe's shifting awareness came as a result of Astrid's "other-ness," and of her different way of seeing the world. Moreover, through his misadventures with Ellen and Astrid, Joe is forced to recognize that the heretofore masculine space of the west—wide, expansive, open to mythic projection—is in fact inhabited and occupied by Others. The space that Turner inscribed is revealed to be fantasy.

But perhaps the most devastating example of McGuane's exploration of how the women of Deadrock destabalize the various masculine fantasies of the men occurs in *Nobody's Angel*. Here, McGuane's hero Patrick Fitzpatrick, suffering from "bouts of sadness-for-no-reason," struggles to come to terms with his sister Mary's failing mental health and eventual death (61).

As a persistent figure in Patrick's life, perhaps even more so after her death, Mary in many ways embodies the wreckage engendered by generations of rugged individuals. Like Patrick, Mary must suffer the absurdity of their grandfather, who obsesses on appearing in *Hondo's Last Move*, a film being shot in Deadrock. Though their father has died in the spectacular plane crash, their grandfather is a "type"—a cowboy warrior—who seemingly represents a comic version of all the Fitzpatrick men. This established masculine lineage is seemingly inherited and multigenerational. Before their grandfather, the elder Fitzpatrick, there was his father, who began the family's "absurd relationship to America's affairs of war" and established the army as "handy place of education since the Civil War" (104). Within this context, his death during the Civil War while "driving mules that pulled a Parrot gun into position during the bombardment of Little Round Top" serves as a marker of the "absurd relationship" to violence (104). Moreover, it seems to presage a Fitzpatrick family legacy of "not fitting in" and a disposition toward mental illness, which McGuane implicitly relates to an over-enthusiastic commitment to rugged individualism:

Apart from [their grandfather's] death, there was the tradition of rather perfunctory military service, then, starting at Miles City in 1884, cattle ranching, horse ranching and a reputation of recurring mental illness, persistent enough that it tended to be assigned from one generation to the next. Mary seemed to have been assigned this time. The luckier ones got off with backaches, facial tics, and alcoholism. The family had now lived in this part of Montana for a very long time, and they still did not fit or even want to fit or, in the words of Patrick's grandfather, "talk to just anybody." (103)

As a result, Patrick and Mary, as well as their eccentric grandfather, exist in Deadrock as isolates. As McGuane writes, "They had no one to turn to besides themselves, despite that they didn't get along very well. . . . Only Patrick and Mary with her hoarding mind and their insufferable grandfather were left to show what there had been" (104).

Though Patrick has managed for a time to escape this legacy while commanding tanks in Germany, Mary has no access to such "heroic" roles.[6] Rather, her painfully direct consciousness only seems to intensify her awareness of the absurdity of the Fitzpatrick men's ways. Moreover, her awareness, revealed in telling, laconic moments, seems to function as a critique of "Old West" mythologies and their romanticizing of violence. At one point in the novel, Mary's grandfather reminisces with ironically noted nostalgia about an old Montana man. The grandfather recalls an old "Virginian who used to do the nicest kind of long work," but then "would get tanked up and fight with a knife," and how "old Warren Butterfield killed him and buried him past the Devils Slide" (55). Mary's response is characteristically direct. "Kill, shoot, whack, stab, chop," she says to both Patrick and his father, accurately lampooning and summarizing the "romantic" past of all the male Fitzpatricks and the nation at large (55).

Beyond this, Mary seems to understand that her father's "strong-silent" type of masculine presence has had certain devastating effects. In fact, she seems to have internalized much of the pathology inherent in Fitzpatrick family history. When discussing the plane wreck of their father, her comments to Patrick prove telling:

"Mary, remember the jet that crashed last winter up in the Arkansas?" "Yes . . ." She stared at the ranch yard as Patrick glided toward the turnaround at the barn. "Well,

I found it with my binoculars. I could see a wing sticking out of the snow, just the tip. It's behind Monitor Peak. I went up there." She coddled her satchel. "One book I wouldn't take to a desert island is a family album." "Now, what's that supposed to mean?" he asked. Mary turned and looked full at him. "It means," she said, "that Daddy's not in that plane." (30)

As Mary's ambiguous remark suggests, her father was not in the plane, but rather alive within her own, fragmented psyche.

After Mary's death, Patrick too is ultimately unable to escape the past. Her death becomes a constant reminder of a pained personal history. Before she dies, during a midnight visit, Mary reveals a fantasy. She adopts her brother's favorite persona, Marion Easterly, an "imagined" girlfriend invented years before by the adolescent Patrick. She speaks through the darkness toward Patrick:

"I am Marion Easterly," said the voice. "You never let me exist. I am not allowed to let you rest. But one night at the proper phase of the moon, a neither-here-nor-there phase of the famous moon, I will arise in the face of our mother and our father and I will be real and you will not have been sent away to school and the proper apologies will be made and you still will have won the roping drunk at the Wilsall rodeo; and all, all will be acceptable. . . . Take away the offending years . . . , for they have ruined us with crumminess and predictability. (119)[7]

The voice of Marion Easterly becomes a voice of resistance, marking the refusal of the Other to accept erasure. A constructed presence—a presence feuding with the "absence presence" of the father—she fights for inclusion within the masculine territory. Even her name subverts narrative tradition. The conventional "Mary" is replaced with the sexually ambiguous "Marion," while "Easterly" notes her rejection of the narrative territory. This colonial Other, found emblematically in Marion Easterly, is an Other noted by Bhabba in his discussion of the colonial. This Other "demands an articulation of forms of difference" that are notably gendered and racialized. It strives for recognition. For McGuane, this colonial discursive voice—seeking to unseat patriarchal power—is typically female and finds clear expression in the subversive ghost of Marion Easterly.

The novel fittingly concludes with Patrick leaving Deadrock for good. Town rumor has it that Patrick lives in Madrid, with "an American named Marion Easterly; and that when she was with him, he was a bit of a black-out drinker" (227). McGuane's final comment correspondingly underscores that Mary and her passing has radically destabilized Patrick's world, destroying any possibility of a "coherent" life in "the last best place."

And a River Runs through It

In "Seasons through the Net," an essay paying homage to the semimystical Montana ritual of fly fishing, McGuane admits that his primary motivation for relocating his family to river lined Montana was its famous trout. McGuane attributes his trout obsession to the fishing stories he'd read in men's magazines as a boy:

> The thing is this: my trout memories precede my sighting of a trout. They go way back to a time when, inflamed to angling by rock bass and perch, I read hunting and fishing magazines and settled upon trout as the only fish worthy of my ability. Also the broadbill swordfish. I had examined the Rockwell Kent illustrations in my father's copy of Moby Dick. I didn't for the moment see what I could do about the white whale. . . . Finally I fished for trout in ways other than my fantasy and for many ruinous years haunted Michigan's cheerful trout rivers. Now . . . I [was] loath to confess [I'd] moved family, bag and baggage, to Montana for the sake of, well, not even a mammal. (117)

Indeed, Montana's status as synonymous with nonpareil fly fishing has become a commonplace, the result of countless historical narratives as well as a number of recent famous ones.

In *Trout Fishing in America* (1967), for instance, the late Montanan Richard Brautigan playfully invoked Montana fly fishing to muse about not only the vagaries of American life, but also its absurd mysteries and troubling complexities. For Brautigan trout fishing develops as an activity inextricable with a man's life in the West. As imaged in *Trout Fishing in America*, however, while seemingly holding the promise of a ritual space outside the problems of daily living, trout fishing ultimately emerges as tainted through its connection to a darker West. In an emblematic vignette, for example, Brautigan's narrator begins by recalling Hemingway's suicide, and then has a strange conversation with a mythic character, named Trout Fishing in America.[8] Recalling his painful boyhood years with his stepfather, the narrator ends up focusing on the memory of solitary mornings in Great Falls, Montana, where he fished and didn't have to do anything serious "like growing up." Later, the conversation references the Lewis and Clark expedition, and how "they went fishing below the falls and caught half a dozen trout, good ones, too, from sixteen to twenty-three inches long" (148).

As Brautigan's allusions suggest, trout-fishing-as-escape is indeed resonant with "not having to do anything serious like growing up." But like Hemingway's Jake Barnes in *The Sun Also Rises* (1926), who spends an idyllic week escaping to the streams of Spain in effort to evade the unpleasant realities of his existence, fishing's eternal promise of release seems to fall short and fails Brautigan as well. In the same manner, beside the river, Brautigan's narrator is inevitably brought back to the sad circumstances of his life. Similarly, in his famous *A River Runs through It* (1976), Norman Maclean elegantly complicates the sacred in fishing by associating it in some ways with a remote father and the violence inherent in a western life. As Maclean writes, Paul's famous right hand wields the rod in sublime rhythm:

Rhythm was just as important as color and just as complicated. It was one rhythm superimposed upon another, our father's four-count rhythm of the line and wrist being still the base rhythm. But superimposed upon it was the piston two count of his arm and the long overriding four count of the completed figure eight of his reversed loop. (8)

But the same hand that rhythmically works the rod ultimately contributes to Paul's violent death through fist fighting. Fishing, masculine rite that it is, is contaminated for Maclean by its association with the more destructive elements of this same identity. The rhythms of the river, a space seemingly beyond Paul's blackouts and fighting, is ultimately tinged by violence, by mystery.

In McGuane's Deadrock novels, the mysteries of trout fishing similarly are associated with spiritual and psychic ambiguity. Fishing alludes not only to a nostalgic discursive past—the place fishing holds in narratives, the westering experience, from Lewis and Clark's narrative to the fiction of Hemingway, Faulkner, and Maclean, and countless others—but also to its own problematic status as a trope associated with male escape, separation, and rugged individualism. In McGuane's fiction, Montana's famous rivers thus initially seem to hold out the promise of a space outside history, beyond cultural inscriptions. Amid the often breathtaking scenery, however, even the promise of Montana's famous crystalline rivers fail to provide sufficient escape from an increasingly alienating and disturbing world. Alas, McGuane's Deadrock protagonists find that fishing, like other mythic western activities, fails to live up to its promise.

In McGuane's Deadrock, fishing, like ranching and the *mano-y-mano* business world, evolves as a kind of synecdoche, reflective of the entire discursive field. While possessing a definite mystique, it suggests an associative dysfunction. This theme is explored in *Keep the Change* when Joe watches an idyllic scene involving fishing, and it devolves from one of romantic possibility to one of dread. Looking at a man and woman fishing along the "lovely waterland," he first envisions romance, then "reality."

The woman hands the man a paper bag and tells the man: "'If you beat me up like you did last weekend, I ain't going to buy you no more of that'" (51). While this sort of comic undercutting of the romance of fishing exists in all the Deadrock novels, McGuane thematically interrogates fishing and its relation to the mythic West most aggressively in *Something to Be Desired* and *Nothing but Blue Skies*.

In *Something to Be Desired*, the romantic possibility of a "pure" experience associated with fishing ultimately eludes Lucien. Moreover, any possibility of its acquiring a nostalgic caste is subverted through its association with Lucien's nearly parodic "Western" father. Before capitulating to a completely downward spiral, Lucien tries to escape to the pristine environs of his inherited ranch. Initially he believes he can get free from his problematic past. There, afloat, he realizes, "Everything was being sold to guitarists and pants designers. He was going to fish quietly and sweat it out" (61).

From this uneasy beginning, Lucien then goes fishing with his romantic interest, Dee. Again the scene has an idyllic aura. "Aquatic insects drifted from the creek and speckled the windshield of the sedan moving between alternating panels of light, vegetation and sky. The sedan's luster was magnificent with nature's passing show" (60). But later, the sublime is subverted, and fishing's promise of escape passes. Lucien catches "three small cutthroats before turning his attention to the end of his small escape. He thought, I have only myself to blame." He then closes "his fly box with its hundred treasures, and the escape was over" (61). When Lucien returns to the car, he tries to sound upbeat. "I got three fish." Dee responds sarcastically: "Three fish. That's nice. You got three fish. There, it's down. Happy?" (61). Lucien then resigned, pulled back from the "pure" space of watery escape. "Let's find a way to get this over with," he tells Dee seductively. She finally responds, appropriately: "You sickening fuck. I feel like a sewer" (61). The scene serves to mark the corruption of the "pure" waters, and the process that turns them into "sewers." Here, the cause of the corruption is linked both to the romance of fishing and to competition, and to the insistence of the phallus-centered ego.

The scene ultimately foreshadows a larger critique of fishing-as-escape in the novel, which occurs later as Lucien struggles to come to terms with his childhood experiences. When Lucien recovers from a blackout binge, he finds himself reminiscing about a youthful fishing trip he took to the Madison river with his father. Accompanying them was his father's friend, business partner, and drinking companion Ben Rush, who happened also to be a former prizefighter, and another man who worked for them named Andrew McCourtney.

As might be expected, Lucien's memory is not nostalgic, but rather painfully emblematic of his acculturation into the masculine world of his father. On the trip, Lucien befriends McCourtney, who decides not to participate in the ritualistic dissipation associated with such fishing trips. As McGuane writes, McCourtney was "a fragile Irishman who had been shell-shocked, and his face had sudden unwilled movements" (70). He avoided drinking because it "threw him into the Second World War, and he'd screech about booby-trapped German cameras, snipers in bombed chateaus, and law school; he'd flunked his bar examination and become a salesman, working for Lucien's father and Ben Rush" (72). Thus unencumbered by hangover, McCourtney would arise early each morning, "while the other two slept," wake "young Lucien to take him out for the morning mayfly hatch; and Lucien would be completely and unquestionably happy" (73).

Eventually however, for reasons that would forever remain mysterious to Lucien, his father and Rush come up with a prank to subvert McCourtney's relationship with Lucien. One night while drunk, Rush and Lucien's father takes Lucien aside and tell him: "When McCourtney comes around in the morning, tell him you're not in the mood to fish; tell him to find somebody else" (73). Uneasily, Lucien complies, rupturing his relationship with the sensitive McCourtney, who might have provided a different and less dangerous masculine model. As a result, McCourtney eventually leaves the abusive men, and Lucien's memory of fishing thus leads him to an understanding of its ritualistic part in an entangled western upbringing by a drunken father. Rather than promising a life of escapes, fishing carries with it the corrosive residue of the past. His father and Ben Rush's childish prank—resonant with Brautigan's narrator's desire to not have to "grow up," while seemingly harmless, is thus associated with the "dark side" of rugged individualism, an individualism rooted in the competition and resistance to difference. Lucien's memory of fishing with his father haunts him. Andrew McCourtney's remoteness, and implied mental slippage, in turn, "last Lucien a lifetime" (73) and perpetuate his own sense of free floating dislocation in the West.

In *Nothing but Blue Skies*, McGuane explores the connection between the nostalgic past and its association with the ritual of fishing. Early in the novel, the beleaguered Frank Copenhaver, reeling from poor life decisions and a divorce from his wife Gracie, decides to escape to a Deadrock river with his old friend Phil. Like Frank, Phil suffers from a failed marriage.

Though the trip begins auspiciously and reverently enough—Frank begins the day by looking at "a silvery gleam along the ridge of the Lutheran church" (75)—it quickly erodes. On the river with Phil, Frank attempts to remain buoyant, even though Phil insists on talking about his failed marriage and the general crumminess of things. Frank tells him that when he fishes he tries to "stop thinking about everything else" (81).

But soon the scenario dissolves further, and by the end of the day, both Frank and Phil struggle to maintain spirits in the face of their ongoing dialectics about life in the West. When, in the end, Phil rather pathetically announces that "'if we didn't have trout fishing, there'd be nothing you could really call pure in our lives at all'," it provides an ironic gloss (82). Fishing is anything but pure. Rather, it somehow is deeply implicated in a vision that has ceased to function for both men.

These early scenes provide a prelude for what turns out to be a much more specific interrogation of fishing occurring later, when Frank accompanies his college-age daughter Holly on a series of fishing trips on his idyllic ranch. The subtext of these trips has been shaped not only by Frank's broken marriage and the fact that he has decided to sell the family ranch, but by Holly's relationships with a series of men, in particular, a perverse hyperwesterner called Layne Lawlor. Until recently, Holly has been an ideal child. Not only was she an excellent student, but she could "out fish" Frank. Layne Lawlor, though, truly causes Frank to worry over the messages he has imparted to Holly.

On their first outing, however, Frank knows nothing of Lawlor. Holly's previous boyfriend had been a similar type, an "avid, excited young man" who seemed to think his being a fisherman covered everything (148). He'd taken that "he and Frank had known each other of years; it was part of the angling camaraderie" (149). Frank, of course, despised him, as he eventually will Lawlor. Holly's attraction to almost parodic images of himself leads Frank to "speak through fishing" (149). He uses this symbolic language in an attempt to get Holly to understand the fallibility of a hard-core westerner view, which he is only gradually coming to recognize himself. Appropriately, their conversation centers around Frank's father. Following Holly's question, "'What kind of fisherman was Grandpa?'" Frank replies, "'Honestly?'" and then tells her "'Not very good.'" This of course surprises Holly, who remembered him only as "fishing constantly." Frank then tells her: "Your grandfather's problem was that he didn't trust anything or anyone but himself. He had to have a hold of things. A good trout fisherman has to understand a slack line. A slack line is everything. That was too much for Grandpa. If that line wasn't tight, he believed it was out of control. I never knew him to catch a big fish. Big fish are caught on a slack line" (149).

The myth of patriarchal fishing superiority, as contained in the notion of a "hard" controlling line being more effective, is shattered.

Rippling here within the semiotics of fishing, is Frank's—indeed, McGuane's—critique of rugged individualism, as well as the trope of fishing and its relation to violent and intractable versions of masculine behavior. Curiously, Frank has come to recognize that Holly's strange acculturation in the West has cast her as a kind of feminist-cum-sportsman, a perverse embodiment of his own previously skewed beliefs. Ultimately, the text and thus the reader are forced to confront the difficult and historic associations with fishing. For while fishing is sometimes acclaimed as the most beautiful masculine art, lying at the very heart of the American mythology of nature, and while the fish is regularly associated with emblems of salvation, the semiotic of fishing possesses a more complicated legacy.

In Hemingway's *Old Man and the Sea* (1952), the protagonist is forced to read his failure to catch a fish—his failure thus to produce a commercial product—as a commentary on his masculinity, making the fishing rod a kind of phallic extension. This conflation of fishing with masculine sexuality is continued by Brautigan when, in *Trout Fishing in America*, the narrator celebrates the process of fishing by seducing his wife on the riverbank. This cult of excessive masculinity, of course, proves disastrous for both Hemingway and Brautigan.

But the association of the phallus within the mythology of western sportsmanship lies deeper. Remarking on his code of rugged Individualism, renowned fisher and hunter Teddy Roosevelt cautioned his followers to "walk softly but carry a big stick," thereby linking the phallus with the accoutrements of sports, and finally with policy of expansionism. Dedicating his novel to his friend Roosevelt and Roosevelt's masculine doctrine, Owen Wister wrote about "the Virginian," an unformed callow youth who must discover his own masculinity through the phallus—that is, through sexuality and its emblem of the gun. The phallic object represents, of course, the fetishized penis, the object that provides the most potent physical and symbolic presence for the absent father. The fishing rod and the gun, like the "big stick" of rugged individualism, act as "the scene of fetishism [that] is also the scene of reactivism and repetition of primal fantasy" (Bhabba, "The Other Question," 80).

McGuane comments on these masculine objects—the phallus itself ("it's harder than Chinese arithmetic'" mutters Frank [32]), the gun, the fishing rod and finally the ever-extending multinational corporations—for all of these structure and necessarily corrupt the discourses of the West. Writes Homi Bhabha, commenting on this problem: "The arbiter of this nationalist/naturalist ethic is the bearer of a peculiar, visible invisibility (some call it the phallus)" (59). Sometimes comic, sometimes affectionate, the patriarchal code with its emblematic and fetishizing association with fishing must ultimately be controlling and finally untenable. Fetishized, the diversion itself becomes one more manifestation of the father. This fear haunts Frank as he fishes.

Later, the fear becomes realized when he meets Lawlor. He sees his daughter approaching with "a gaunt figure with a shock of gray curls, wearing a three-piece suit and lace-up cowboy packer boots" (206). As Frank learns, Lawlor, roughly his own middle age, is a leading figure in "We, Montana," a group of activists obsessed with barring "outsiders" and "infiltrators" from Montana and with connections to "Posse Comitatus, as well as the radical tax protestors of the Dakotas" (206).

Lawlor and his political colleagues reference an alternate vision of Montana, one that displaces the romantic allure of "the last best place" that Frank (and McGuane) envisions. Instead, Lane Lawlor, "dressed as Frank's grandfather," represents the forces of conservative politics, unhindered capitalism, and the repressive history of the Old West. Lawlor, as McGuane's text implies, is as much a product of the western cosmology and heritage as the more free spirited Frank. As Richard Slotkin suggests, in his *Gunfighter Nation*, the contemporary ethos of rugged individualism in business, as well the resurgence of right-wing militia and activists have their roots in Turner's frontier hypothesis. Reading the election of Ronald Reagan as indicative of this national regressive Slotkin argues:

[t]he Reagan version of "supply-side" economics represents a recrudescence (with modifications) of the Turnerian approach to economic development. In its original or primary formulation, Turner's Frontier Hypothesis held that the prosperity and high growth rates of the American economy had been made possible by the continual expansion of the Frontier . . . "Reaganomics" in effect proposed a tertiary Turnerism, in which the multiplication and manipulation of financial capital replaces . . . agrarian commodities. (645–46)

Slotkin goes on to note that even such concepts as "trickle-down theory" were rooted in Turner's hypothesis, and he adds that the term, "frontier" enjoyed under Reagan (especially within financial discourse) "its widest currency since 1960–63" (645–46). This Turnerian ideology, maintains Slotkin, inevitably has resulted in giant agri-business interests, multinational corporations and deregulation, as well as in the increase in militia-like organizations.[9] This so-called New West is clearly evident today in the vast ranches of such personalities as media-mogul Ted Turner. Lawlor is a representation of this "New West" and is, as much as Frank, a part of its inherited topography.

In the context of his rethinking of his own life in the not so "unsolved" distance of the west, Frank understands Lawlor as representative of the dangers of an unbridled nostalgia for the "old" ways. From Frank's perspective, Lawlor's neoconservatism and sense of self-righteousness is resonant with the former manifest destiny and fantasies of a monolithic, monochromatic West, whose repressive history has ties to Frank's father. When Lawlor announces he is from Fort Benton, "right where the history of Montana began," Frank replies: "Oh, the white history of Montana" (205). Later, when Frank sees Lawlor's picture in the paper, Lawlor correspondingly appears as a parodic, modern-day incarnation of the Old West hero/destroyer/father.

It is this image of Lawlor as emblematic of the Old West, and Holly's attraction to him, that ultimately forms the subtext for Frank and Holly's ill-fated trip to their former fishing site. Prior to the trip, thanks in part to Holly's affinity for Lawlor, Frank's fondness for fishing has already faded. Alone, fishing on an isolated stream, Frank envisions both the scene and the process as hellish. He wonders "how Dante had failed to perfect one of his circles for the philandering sportsman, ravaged by his own hounds, flogged with his own fishing poles, dancing over buckshot" (234). And when Frank and Holly arrive at the site of their former fishing trip, his vision proves prescient.

Initially, however, the occasion of fishing is charged with nostalgia. As they make their way through the seemingly fecund foliage, Frank anxiously pulls out his "thirty-year-old bamboo rod" and opens a "battered aluminum fly box that had been a gift from Gracie twenty years before." He ties on a "1930's Blackfoot River" fly, a "favorite . . . which a friend in Missoula had tied for him" (280). But as they hunt for their old spot, it slowly dawns on Frank that something is unfamiliar. He asks Holly: "Are we lost?" They soon discover they indeed are "lost," that the nostalgic space of the romantic river has been displaced and made untenable. Prefigured by Frank's earlier vision of fishing-as-hell, the once familiar site has lost its idyllic-ness. Further investigation reveals a "broad dyke for impounding water. Here the ruptured earth . . . bore blade marks and the impoundment yard continued to fill." Nearby, "serviceberry bushes and aspens half submerged were still alive. Bright new aluminum pipes for advance irrigation system were pyramided on low wagons" (281).

As suspected, Frank is ultimately able to attribute the problem to Lawlor and his associates. Frank deems Lawlor "the sort of fascist windbag that produces this kind of activity" (281). As the scene suggests, Lawlor's absurd expression of a particular form of masculinity ironically has the effect of destroying any possibility for the persistence of the nostalgic space of the river.

Like Maclean's "haunted" waters, McGuane's rivers similarly represent a delicate space. While holding the promise of sublime release, they are also discursively associated with the problematic aspects of the romantic West. As a postmodern, McGuane is acutely self-conscious about these associations, and the Deadrock novels reflect an ongoing critique of their persistence and power within the mythic context of Montana as "the last best place."

Re: Rivers

As McGuane's cigar-smoking fishermen cast their lines out across the silver water, they are painfully aware that this encoding of male space is potentially dangerous. Just as McGuane's Frank is ultimately saved quite literally by "Grace," for Grace is his estranged wife, McGuane's texts posit that meaning and salvation must be found in some alternate dialogue outside masculine discourse. The tragedy of McGuane's West is that the narrow male world must finally culminate in violence and destruction. It is a prolonged fishing expedition gone awry. Thus, McGuane's texts seemingly ponder Bhabha's concern that phallic fascination and privilege raise sinister questions. For, as Bhabha points out, operating within the sphere of the absent present father—within the periphery of a presence that is known and missed—there is a persistent desire to find renewed representation of this gendered ideology. "What happens," Bhabha asks rhetorically: "[w]hen the phallic structure of *amor patriae* turns into an anxious ambivalance . . . ? What kind of atavism emerges in the political sphere when that "relation of antecedence" which is traditionally associated with patriarchal precedence is challenged at the very root of its desire? Can democracy turn demonic in the service of a nation through observing the imperatives of phallic respect?" (60). Bhabha's question is at least in large part rhetorical, for, indeed, much of his writing suggests ways in which western patriarchal democracy turns "demonic." The landscape created by McGuane and his fellow Montana authors reflects this demonic possession. As its patriarchal origins are interrogated, Bhabba's theoretical point finds narrative representation.

Like the other texts discussed in this book, McGuane's novels seek to remake the American West, and to allow other, often marginalized, voices to subvert the reified structure of patriarchy. For McGuane, it is women in particular who—because of the phallic orientation of western narrative—necessarily become agents of subversion. For McGuane, women are the Other who must constantly seek to unseat the patriarch. Because of their gender, women lie outside the traditional warring discourse of fathers and sons, and thus they have a sporting chance at success.

Even in McGuane's texts, just as predicted by Bhabba, the fetishes and power of patriarchy continually endeavor to reassert themselves. But in the small breaks, in the moment wherein the father is (even temporarily) disempowered, narrative expression changes course. The Montana writers offer another view of these discursive alterations, offering a revamped and ironic West. This is a new narrative West, one that challenges the traditional mythologies and borders. Bhabba writes of an "anxious ambivalence," of a mood that threatens the legitimacy of the father, recasting narrative and political possibility. It is within Bhabha's "anxious ambivalence" that McGuane's texts operate, comically seeking the "absence presence" of the father and simultaneously acknowledging that to find this presence—even fleetingly—is dangerous.

Notes

1. In this same essay, "Montana Renaissance," Kittredge writes of the desire—however absurd or impossible—to seek and find "a good place in which to conduct a good life" (765). But Kittredge's literary "renaissance," that began to occur in Montana in the late 1970s, was paralleled by another more sinister movement. Right wing Aryan supremacists, militia members, and most recently the so-called far-right "Freemen" began also to struggle to reclaim the state as an appropriate site for a reconstituted, rearmed masculine pathology. McGuane's work, along with that of Richard Ford, Jim Harrison, and Rick DeMarinis, sheds light on these events and movements.

2. Since the beginnings of this century, the West has provided a background for commercial advertisement and has in this way nearly become a commodity itself. During the first decades of the century western scenery provided a backdrop for the sale of guns and railway tickets. After World War II, the rugged spaces of Montana and Idaho became synonymous with the "Marlboro Man" and the "masculine" (even phallic) trope of smoking. In more recent, post–Ronald Reagan years, the West has been associated with new commercial trends in fashion, cuisine, and music.

3. See Homi Bhabha's essay, "Are You a Man or a Mouse?" *Constructing Masculinity* (edited by Berger, Wallis, and Watson. New York: Routledge, 1995).

4. The elder Fitzpatrick's work for Boeing is interesting, in light of the fact that McGuane, finally, suggests that the most far-reaching representations of patriarchy are found in large corporations, like Boeing. For McGuane, in the postmodern world, these super corporations become a kind of metafather.

5. This same desire to remasculinize and reassert an older topos of manhood, against the feared "feminine" forces, is discussed in Ann Douglas's *The Feminization of American Culture* (New York: Alfred A. Knopf, 1977).

6. Again, Patrick's escape into the military is simply an escape into another patriarchal "family." Like large corporations, the military operates here as a metaphor for patriarchal control and its necessary and recurring cult of action and violence.

7. Like many of the names used by McGuane, Marion Easterly is coded. The name "Marion" makes her the alter-ego of Mary Fitzpatrick, but it also associates her with the Virgin. As her surname and speech suggest though, this virgin is an unhappy, restive icon, more at home with the images and trends that originate in the east than with any western topography. She is not a "westerly"—a common wind of the west.

8. It is interesting to note that "Trout Fishing in America" retains his mythic power. In recent years, a young man successfully went to court and changed his name officially to "Trout Fishing in America."

9. For an expanded discussion of this political phenomenon, see Richard Slotkin's *Gunfighter Nation*, most particularly the segment, "Back in the Saddle Again? The Reagan Presidency and the Recrudescence of the Myth," pp. 643–54. Slotkin further argues that out of this mythological resurgence comes Reagan, Reagan's cold war policy, and the image of the "evil empire." This is further accompanied by the cinematic genre of vigilantism, the distrust of "big" government, the codified support for "states' rights," and the fear that aliens and extraterrestrials are about to destroy American hegemony. Writes Slotkin, "the political successes of the Reagan and Bush administrations suggest that in the 1980s there was indeed a renewal of public myth: a general disposition to think mythologically about policy questions, substituting symbol and anecdote for analysis and argument; and a specific revival of the ideological structures of the Frontier Myth." (652).

Works Cited

Anderson, Benedict. *Imagined Communities*. London: Verso, 1991.

Athearn, Robert G. *The Mythic West*. Kansas: University of Kansas Press, 1986.

Bhabha, Homi. "Are You a Man or a Mouse," *Constructing Masculinity*. Berger, Wallis, Watson, editors. London: Routledge, 1995.

———. "The Other Question: Difference, Discrimination and the Discourse of Colonialism," *Out There: Marginalization and Contemporary Cultures*. Cambridge: MIT Press, 1991.

Brautigan, Richard. *Trout Fishing in America*. San Francisco: Four Seasons Foundation, 1967.

Douglas, Ann. *The Feminization of American Culture*. New York: Alfred A. Knopf, 1977.

———. Kittredge, William, and Annick Smith. *The Last Best Place*. Helena: Montana Historical Society Press, 1989.

Maclean, Norman. *A River Runs Through It*. Chicago: University of Chicago Press, 1976.

McGuane, Thomas. *Nobody's Angel*. New York: Random House, 1981.

———. *An Outside Chance*. New York: Penguin, 1982.

———. *Something to Be Desired*. New York: Vintage, 1984.

———. *Keep the Change*. New York: Vintage, 1989.

———. *Nothing but Blue Skies*. Boston: Houghton Mifflin, 1992.

Slotkin, Richard. *Gunfighter Nation: The Myth of the Frontier in Twentieth-Century America*. New York: Macmillan, 1992.

Tompkins, Jane. *West of Everything*. New York: Oxford University Press, 1992.

Turner, Frederick Jackson. *The Significance of the Frontier in American History*. New York: Continuum, 1963.

Selected Filmography

Fort Apache (1948, Universal). Director: John Ford.
How the West Was Won (1962, Paramount). Director: John Ford.
Shane (1953, Paramount). Director: George Stevens.
Winchester 77 (1950, Universal). Director: Anthony Mann.

CHAPTER EIGHT

Coda—Indians, Cowboys, Others: Performing at the Borders of Postmodernism

The Signifying Frontier

Coyote Kills John Wayne began with the World's Colombian Exposition of 1893, where western historian Frederic Jackson Turner delivered his seminal speech "The Significance of the Frontier in American History," and where Buffalo Bill performed his audacious Wild West Show in which numerous "authentic" Indians performed. In their own ways, both cultural performances reified certain imperial narratives that all the texts assembled here have in one manner or another engaged. Beyond, both cultural performances—Buffalo Bill's panoramic reenactment of the "winning of the west," and the imperialist cultural displays of the exhibition—exemplify the peculiar ways in which performance and spectacle have become synonymous with the frontier since the turn of the century.

In describing the 1893 exposition, Richard Slotkin has noted that the performance of Buffalo Bill's Wild West spectacle at the exposition in fact marked a transformation of the West from a "place" to a "show": "[Buffalo Bill's Wild West], despite its battery of authentications. . . . , wrote "history" by conflating it with mythology. [Buffalo Bill's] re-enactments were not re-creations but reductions of complex events. . . . If the Wild West was a "place" rather than a "show," then its landscape was a mythic space in which past and present, fiction and reality, could coexist; a space in which history, translated into myth, was re-enacted as ritual" (69). For Slotkin, this staging of history as fictive performance, which continues in different ways to this day, provides an illustration of the imperialism inherent in visions of the American frontier.

But against this notion of the frontier as a universalized, stable conceptual category, *Coyote Kills John Wayne* has attempted to explore the ways in which the very idea of the frontier and the West has been contested by a range of contemporary fictions. These fictions explore a transcultural and largely deconstructed frontier—a frontier that seems always to have existed as a kind of socio-political construct.

At the same time, postmodernism has been read as a matrix, a historically emergent set of strategies that sometimes has occasioned inquiries into the constructedness of identity and the role of semiotics in creating discursive formations. Such disruptive strategies potentially can call into question the very notion of fixed identities, imperial narratives, borders, and, of course, the frontier itself. Yet the historic persistence of the frontier as a cultural and literary trope cannot be underestimated or theorized away. Historically reified, it remain a historic and political site against which many artists work. It is a mobile shifting border, indefinable, constructed, deconstructed, and always a spectral presence.

Postmodern theory is not necessary to explicate the texts that subvert the reified notion of western dance in the elusive spaces between the frontier's borders. Indeed, it would be a mistake to seek to theoretically corral or define the various texts discussed in this book. But the dance between theory, history, and the texts of the borderlands provides a way to understand the process of resistance, reconfiguration, and semiotic appropriation. This dance is about the process of how borders are drawn and erased, and redrawn and again revised. While postmodern theory may not be necessary in order to read the texts of the borderlands, these narratives instruct us in how to apprehend the larger postmodern landscape. They provide a lens through which we perceive the shifting, always reconstituting cultural space of the contemporary world. In what some have taken to calling the culture wars— the struggles to redefine notions of identity, mythology, and literature— these frontier narratives find particular significance.

The dance between theory and narrative is a dialectic. Postmodern theory elucidates this dialectic and sheds critical light on fiction. Fiction unmasks theory. But fiction—story—finally speaks for itself. And so it is worth repeating here that the aim of this book has not been to demonstrate how postmodernism stages these texts—particularly those by native writers— but how these texts perform postmodernism.

Through story and through theorizing acts, the frontier—so clearly defined for Turner—becomes ephemeral, a chimera whose trace has dramatic cultural consequences. How then do we understand frontier and border, ideas that we acknowledge are not static, ideas that we deconstruct, ideas

that continue, in the words of Derrida, to persist in their spectral haunting? It may be that the borderlands, with all their vexing questions concerning hybridity, identity, nationality, and history, must be performed,
rather than defined.

Border Performances

It is interesting that in this millennial moment we watch the reassertion of
the West as a performative space, with the frontier persisting as a trope that
is endlessly remapped and subverted. During the past decade the wild west
show and the rodeo have enjoyed a rapid and renewed popularity. (There
are at this writing dinner theaters that like Buffalo Bill reenact the West,
and the national rodeo circuit is followed by ever-increasing numbers). But
more significantly, the staging of the frontier has shifted, and the borderlands are interrogated not only by mainstream *aficianados* but by those
groups that were once defined by their marginal positions vis-à-vis the
frontier. There are today gay rodeos and western shows that use camp and
irony to reinvigorate an old theme. Initially popular in southern
California's inland empire and Texas, gay line dancing has become a way to
subvert and reinvent the seemingly rigid masculine mythologies of the
west and to create some alternative masculine space. But whereas line
dancing in its more original form concerned the markings of distinct codes
and borders, this revived line dance marks a mobile place of play, a place
where gender and space are constantly and freely reconfigured. The dance
reflects the steps and costumes of its earlier incarnation, but it reperforms
itself, probing identity, masculinity, and the hybridity of the frontier.

The choreographing of the frontier continues in numerous other cultural venues, through other border-negotiating gestures, made by those who
occupy this slipping and liminal space. In *Chicano Narrative: The Dialectics of
Difference* (1990), Ramón Salidivar discusses the historic resistance encoded in folk music and dance, using Americo Paredes's study regarding
resistance and the *corrido* as a point of departure. Salidivar expands the argument to include a consideration of *conjunto* music and its position on the
borders of hegemonic culture. *Conjunto* is itself a hybrid art form, originat-
ing on the borders of the American southwest and incorporating the instruments and sounds of European immigrants. As Salidivar notes elsewhere, *conjunto* today enjoys a renewed popularity. *Billboard Magazine* has
devoted space to the musical genre, commenting on the various gold and

platinum records awarded to contemporary *conjunto* artists. The musical gestures of the *conjunto*, like other hybrid arts, performs what Salidivar has termed the "Hispanic diaspora"—a migratory space defined by notions of identity, history, and borders.

In a similar vein, poet and cultural critic Ruben Martinez describes the emergence of a new Latino and *mestizaje* dance craze, a craze that first occurred in Los Angeles in the early 1990s. Moving to the beat of *quebradita*, a "fast" and "tinny" sound rooted in nineteenth-century Sinaloa, young Latino immigrants and Chicanos dance into the night, dressed in the "western" inspired garb of chaps, snakeskin, Stetsons, and vinyl boots (Martinez 12). As Martinez notes, these "new American cowboys" represent a kind of "cultural revolution," as they illustrate the emergence of a new, hybridic Los Angeles (10). Martinez interprets this new fashion in dance as a performative form of cultural resistance that responds to recent anti-immigrant rhetoric and legislation. Though the dance has its roots in border ballads and traditional *vaquero* culture, it also highlights the postmodern reappropriation of the traditional hegemonic, Reaganesque codings of "the cowboy" in American culture. Amid this social space, "cowboy" is newly encoded within the political context of *vaquero*, and the gestures of the new, leather-dressed, bangle-wearing, Latino, urban "cowboy" can be viewed as a celebratory dance of resistance replete with metamessages.

Performance artist Guillermo Gomez-Pena has for the last twenty-some years also confronted issues concerning marginalization, representation, and the West. Born in Mexico City, Pena operates internationally as a "migrant performance artist," a nomadic provocateur whose art inherently emerges from the conflicted, hybrid space of globalization. Pena occupies a space of new borders glossed by the historical presence of old lines of demarcation, such as the U.S.-Mexican border in the San Diego area where exploitive free-trade corporate practices flourish amid transcultural tensions (Pena 5–18). For Pena, the U.S.-Mexican border is both political and semiotic; it is a site that facilitates oppression and false impression, particularly when habitually viewed from the perspective of the United States. Confrontational and often hilarious, Pena's performances often blend high and low aspects of postmodern United States' popular culture with traditional and contemporary aspects of Mexican, Latin American, and Indian cultures in an effort to deconstruct the familiar binary categories often associated with imperialism. As a "migrant" critic who works from many sides of many borders, Pena advocates a conceptual remapping of conventional Anglo and frontier paradigms: "I oppose the sinister cartography of the New World Order with the conceptual map of the New World Border—a great trans- and intercontinental border zone, a place in which no center remains. It's all margins, meaning there were no "others," or better said, the only true "others" are those who resist fusion, mestizaje, and cross-cultural dialogue. In this utopian cartography, hybridity is the dominant culture" (7).

Given that Buffalo Bill's Wild West "modern" spectacles clearly played an important role in theatrically and performatively fostering United States' imperialism, Pena's postmodern performance pieces can be understood as counter-spectacles that unmask the ways in which border discourses have functioned within colonial contexts. Ironic and hyperaware of the constructed nature of such notions as "the American West," "the United States' frontier," and a single, hegemonic "America," Pena's work thus reframes identities and subjectivities within the visible nexuses of power and discourse. In a performance called "Year of the White Bear," for example, Pena and collaborators parody what Pena calls the museum "blockbuster multicultural shows" by creating "museum" shows that feature antianthropologist displays (Pena 99). In these shows, Pena reverses the tendency of anthropologists to exoticize pre-Columbian cultures by creating displays that often view indigenous peoples as objects existing out of time. The "Year of the White Bear" entailed the creation of what Pena calls a "fictional center"—wherein the so-called exotic occupies the position of the familiar, as the dominant culture is pushed to the margins (Pena 99). As Pena states, "[W]e (re)created 'an excavation site of tourists from Wisconsin, after being raided by angry locals,' and a 'British collector's room' with his 'secret collection' of stolen indigenous artifacts, revealing his interracial sexual fantasies" (99).

In truly spectacular fashion, the epic "Borderama" perhaps best represents Pena's penchant for counter-spectacle. Incorporating local "involuntary performance artists" such as "street performers, rappers, wrestlers, and/or local media celebrities," "Borderama" approximates a postpunk apocalyptic deconstruction of all border mythologies "separating" North and South America. Within a haze of neon light and amid a mélange of disturbing images, the performance features the mutating presence of a cellist, a naked *Zapatista* (with a black ski mask), wrestlers, skinheads, anthropologists, punks, *choalas* revolutionaries, and various historical figures. The corresponding "narrative" of the performance revolves around staged episodes including the "Identity Escape Act," "An Exercise in Reversed Anthropology," and "Free-trade Sex Auction" (Pena 127–54). Through a series of surreal vignettes that nearly defy description, Pena's theatrics explore imperialist Anglo stereotypes of Latin cultures. Viewers, warned that they will not witness "your average feel-good multi-culti piece," are ultimately left to consider their own complicity in creating oppressive political borders and racialized conceptual frontiers.

Luiseno Indian James Luna, who has performed with Guillermo Pena, has also produced his own performance works in attempting to articulate a counter-narrative in opposition to the familiar western stories about Indians. An artist and poet living within the borderlands of a number of reservations in northern San Diego county, Luna creates installations and performance pieces that correspondingly investigate the cost associated with hybrid identity. For Luna, western narratives of Otherness extend across tribal cultures, often resulting in conflict and despair for "mixed-bloods." In "Half-Indian, Half-Mexican," Luna's narrator explains his own mixed bloodlines, and then describes his hybrid self as "half giving" and "half selfish," "a self made up of many things" (*Sounds* 32). Luna's textual "I" ultimately grounds his hybrid identity in a personal sense of self that must exist beyond the narratives of blood:

> I do not have to be anything for anybody but myself.
> I have survived long enough to find this out.
> I am forty-one years old and am happy with
>   my whole—self.
> Don't let your children wait so long. (*Sounds* 32)

Indeed, much of Luna's performance art deals with "ethnographic" and historically constructed definitions of "Indian-ness," and how such definitions and assumptions impact the "lived-lives" of contemporary native Americans. Identity for Native Americans and Others who inhabit the borderlands is not comprised of "fixed" ethnographic classifications, but must instead be drawn from the ever-mutating positions emergent within the fluid cultural and historical contexts existing beyond westernized ethnographic narratives.

In "On Collecting Art and Culture," James Clifford comments on the connections between "marginalized" identities, ethnography, and a seemingly distinctive western impulse to collect and classify cultures. Recognizing that "collections embody hierarchies of value, exclusions, rule-governed territories of the self," Clifford views ethnographic narratives as forms of "culture collecting," whose fetishizing of the "authentic" represents an important component in the production of "Western identity formation" (*Marginalization* 144):

To see ethnography as a form of culture collecting (not, of course, the only way to see it) highlights the ways that diverse experiences and facts are selected, gathered, detached from their original occasions, and given enduring values in a new arrangement. Collecting—at least in the West, where time is generally thought to be linear and irreversible—implies rescue of phenomena from inevitable historical decay or loss. The collection contains what "deserves" to be kept, remembered and treasured. Artifacts and customs are saved out of time. Anthropological culture collectors have typically gathered what seems "traditional"—what by definition is opposed to modernity. What is hybrid or "historical" as an emergent sense has been less commonly collected and presented as a system of authenticity. (152)

For Clifford, the western preoccupation with "collecting cultures" thus seeks to preserve native (and other) cultures—and by extension, native identities—through institutional practices that reinforce western "assumptions about temporality, wholeness and continuity" (141).

Luna's "Artifact Piece," a "performative installation" accompanied by text, dramatically challenges the historical persistence of ethnographic narratives that seek to "museumize" Native Americans. Viewers who confront Luna's installation encounter Luna's loin-clothed body as he lies face up in a glass-covered display case; his eyes are closed and his body is static. Viewers are quickly reminded of other "Indian" displays that they may have experienced in such institutional spaces as museums and libraries. Luna's display evokes memories of the traditional posed dioramas, featuring perhaps basket-hauling Indians, or a lone "warrior" posed with bow and arrow, or a generic "squaw" trundling a "papoose" and child, or an idyllic communal scene in which exemplary and "noble" natives gather around an "authentic" teepee. But the narrative placards that accompany the displays quickly disrupt such pristine ethnographic fantasies. "The burns on the forearms," viewers learn, were "sustained during days of excessive drinking," after which the displayed Indian "passed out on a campground table" and "fell into a campfire" (Luna 33). "Not until several days later," when the drinking ceased, was the seriousness and pain of the burn realized (33). Later, viewers learn that the Indian on display had been "knocked down" by people "from another reservation," and ultimately "saved by an old man" (33). Hereafter, states the display Indian, he will make it a point "not to be trusting among relatives and other Indians" (33).

Self consciously stark and troubling, Luna's performance implicates viewers again in the nexus of power relations that have perpetuated certain ethnographic representations of native Americans as "noble savages" or as "authentic first Americans" forever preserved within an antique

time. Luna's installation deconstructs the implicit violence of such narratives, particularly as this violence impacts the very body of Native Americans and other marginalized people. Luna's Indian cannot be theorized
away or understood outside the frames of history and imperial oppression.
And while the display ironically reifies certain stereotypes, it simultaneously destabalizes and undermines universalized narratives depicting "authentic" Indians in "authentic" settings. Viewers thus must confront the
specificity of a single Indian "life." Moreover, viewers conditioned habitually to view Native Americans through an ethnographic gaze are compelled to understand the ways in which many historically familiar frontier
narratives involving Indians have institutional corollaries in such collections and displays.

Collecting Indian culture as a static, discreetly contained body is finally
seen as but part of a larger discourse. This discursive and conceptual field
has persistently ignored the reality that Native Americans and reservation
cultures are continually in the process of "becoming." Viewers, Luna
maintains, can no longer safely imagine Indians as they have so often been
depicted in museums, as "still" artifacts. Rather, Luna's piece makes it dramatically clear that such imperial fantasies—which as Clifford maintains
have served to promote western notions of "self"—have left their marks on
Indian bodies and minds.

Ultimately, within the context of *Coyote kills John Wayne*, the image that
persists is not so much Luna's museum piece, but Thomas King's Coyote,
whose own subversive "performance" celebrates the dismantling of historic
stereotypes and oppressive historical narratives of the frontier. Indeed, all of
the texts here challenge conventional ideas of the "West" and "frontier."
These postmodern fictions finally reject binary notions of colonizer and
colonized, victim and exploiter, cowboys and Indians, and instead reflect on
a space of exchange and slippage, a space continually to be re-envisioned.
Indeed, amid this dynamic landscape, Coyote's call reverberates.

Works Cited

Clifford, James. "On Collecting Art and Culture. *Out There: Marginalization and
    Contemporary Cultures.* Ed. Russell Ferguson. Cambridge: MIT Press, 1990.
Luna, James. "Artifact Piece." *The Sounds of Rattles and Clappers: A Collection of New
    California Indian Writing.* Ed. Greg Serris. Tucson: University of Arizona Press,
    1994.
Martinez, Ruben. "The Shock of the New." *Los Angeles Times Magazine*, 30 Jan.
    1994.

Pena, Guillermo Gomez-. *The New World Border: Prophesies, Poems and* Laqueras *for the End of the Century*. San Francisco: City Lights, 1996.

Salidivar, Ramon. *Chicano Narrative: The Dialectics of Difference*. Milwaukee: University of Wisconsin Press, 1990.

Slotkin, Richard. *Gunfighter Nation: The Myth of the Frontier in the Twentieth Century*. New York: Harper Perennial, 1992.

Index